Chefs at Home
DESSERTS

FAVORITE HOME DESSERT RECIPES FROM THE CHEFS
OF RELAIS & CHATEAUX IN NORTH AMERICA

RELAIS &
CHATEAUX.

Published by Chef Books

Network House, 28 Ballmoor, Celtic Court,
Buckingham MK18 1RQ, UK

www.chefmagazine.co.uk

© Chef Books

Printed by MP Printing Limited

ISBN No: 978-1-908202-11-6

Printed in China

Publisher: Peter Marshall
Managing Editor: Shirley Marshall
Editors: Katy Morris, Helen Homes
Designer: Philip Donnelly
Photographers:
Diana Fletcher
Myburgh du Plessis
Peter Marshall

Most chefs crave simple, straight-forward food when they eat at home and and the talented chefs in this new book are no exception.

From Barbara Lynch's Creamy Vanilla Bread Pudding to Jean-George's Chocolate Cake, some of the most brilliant chefs in North America share their favorite desserts when entertaining.

These recipes emphasize seasonality and a sense of place. They reflect the fascinating geographic diversity in cooking styles across our vast continent and open a window into the minds of a fraternity of passionate masters of hospitality.

May they inspire you to entertain your family and friends with greater ease, imagination and confidence. It's reassuring to be reminded that oftentimes simpler can be better.

We look forward to welcoming you to the delicious world of Relais & Châteaux.

Patrick O'Connell

Patrick O'Connell

President of North American Relais & Châteaux Delegations
Chef/ Proprietor of The Inn at Little Washington

RELAIS &
CHATEAUX.

Welcome to *Chefs at Home Desserts*

In 2010, we were privileged to publish *Chefs at Home*, a cookbook with a difference, which showcased a compilation of recipes from the Chefs and Grands Chefs that are part of the family of Relais & Châteaux properties in North America, Mexico and the Caribbean. Widely known for producing exemplary cuisine, these Chefs are regularly complimented on the quality of their food as well as often being showered with accolades. However, even Chefs need to go home, spend time with their families and enjoy the comfort that home brings and this perhaps unsurprisingly includes the pleasures of simple, straightforward food. The essence of the book was to bring together the most cherished at-home dishes that these culinary masters choose to cook for themselves, thus giving you the opportunity to emulate your favorite Chefs by cooking one of their at-home dishes for a quick family meal or impressing with a dinner party.

The book has been a phenomenal success and with this in mind, we present to you this exceptional accompaniment, *Chefs at Home Desserts*, a must have for anyone with a sweet tooth and a slightly decadent nature! Once again, the Relais & Châteaux Chefs come together to share their dessert secrets, from simple recipes handed down through the generations to the more complex, but nevertheless desirable desserts that are just calling out to be recreated and enjoyed.

Every recipe features a personal note from the Chef as to why each dessert has been chosen, sometimes because it simply reminds one of home, sometimes because it represents a great example of a particular season evoking childhood memories and others because it is a favorite, but personal modern twist on grandmother's recipe. Accordingly, the Chefs have ensured, as before, that each recipe is clear and simple to follow, including where possible, a Chef's tip to really help you succeed in producing the very best dessert. Each recipe is from a tried and tested method and even occasionally includes ingredient alternatives, making you feel as if the Chef really is in the kitchen with you. Additionally, they have provided preparation and cooking times to further assist you with the ultimate cooking experience.

All the recipes are beautifully illustrated which will help guide you to creating the perfect dish that looks just as good as it truly tastes. You will find each recipe by alphabetical property order, with a comprehensive index at the back giving you the opportunity to choose the perfect dessert for any occasion.

Chefs at Home Desserts is the ultimate composite dessert book for any aspiring pastry chef or simply for the enthusiastic foodie who knows that any meal must finish on a high note. With *Chefs at Home Desserts*, you too can be part of the Relais & Châteaux family and give your family and friends a dessert to remember. Why not? We are all worth it!

DESSERTS

CONTENTS

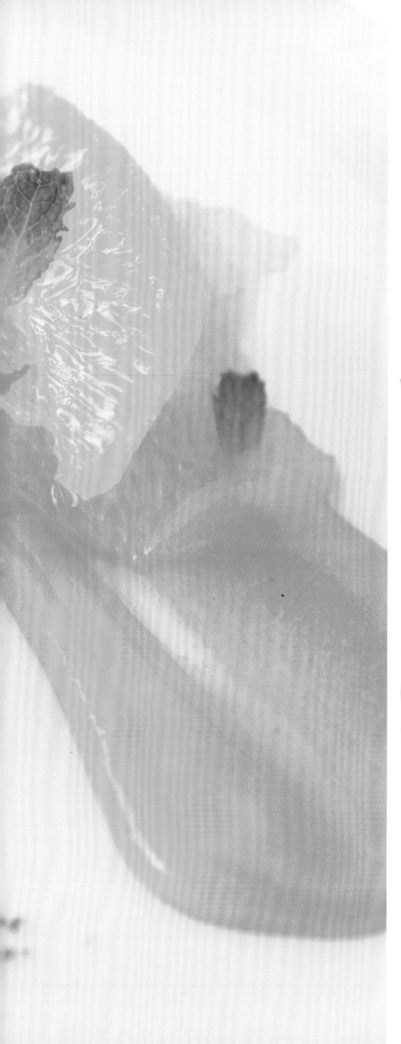

VANILLA PANNA COTTA WITH BASIL MARINATED CITRUS

BY WILLIAM BRADLEY

The tang of citrus, the subtle hint of pepper from the basil, and the silkiness of creamy panna cotta – this combination creates a luscious dessert at any time of the year.

VANILLA PANNA COTTA WITH BASIL-MARINATED CITRUS

BY WILLIAM BRADLEY

Serves 4

Preparation time: 15 minutes
Cooking time: 15 minutes

ingredients

panna cotta:
¾ cup	cold water
½ tsp	powder gelatin
3 cups	heavy whipping cream
1 cup	cane sugar
3	whole vanilla beans

citrus:
1 cup	orange segments
1 cup	grapefruit segments
1 cup	elderflower syrup
4 whole	basil leaves

method

panna cotta:
1. Pour a ¼ cup of cold water into a small custard cup. Sprinkle the gelatin over it and let it stand until the gelatin softens, about 15 minutes. In a small pot bring a ½ cup of water to a boil. Place the cup with the gelatin into the water. Stir until the gelatin dissolves, about 2 minutes. Remove from the heat.
2. Combine the cream and sugar in a heavy saucepot. Stir over a medium heat until the sugar dissolves completely. Remove from the heat and slowly mix in the vanilla beans and gelatin. Divide them up into 4 glass jars and refrigerate for one day before serving.

citrus:
Place the citrus segments, elderflower syrup and basil into a glass mixing bowl. Place in the refrigerator for one day before serving.

to serve:
Plate up as shown.

13

APPLE CIDER DONUTS

BY PAUL LEMIEUX

Every year my family would visit the local apple farm and to this day, apple cider donuts bring back childhood memories. One bite and I am back on that farm, sitting on a bale of hay taking in the rich burgundy and mustard colors of fall.

APPLE CIDER DONUTS

BY PAUL LEMIEUX

Serves: Yields 18 donuts and holes

Preparation time: 15 minutes
Cooking time: 12 minutes

ingredients

donuts:

9 oz	all purpose flour
1 tsp	baking powder
½ tsp	baking soda
½ tsp	Ceylon cinnamon powder
¼ tsp	salt
1 oz	butter
1.7 oz	sugar
1 whole	egg
2 oz	buttermilk
3¼ oz	apple cider syrup or reduce 18oz of apple cider syrup to 3¼ oz

cinnamon mixture:

1 oz	Ceylon cinnamon
6 oz	sugar

Calvados sabayon (yields 2 cups):

1 whole	egg
3	egg yolks
1½ oz	sugar
½ oz + 1 oz	Calvados
1 cup	cream

diced apples:

2 whole	Pink Lady apples, diced
1 oz	sugar
pinch	salt

method

donuts:

1. Sift together the dry ingredients. Cream the butter and sugar with a paddle attachment on a medium speed until light and fluffy, about 3 minutes. Add the egg, scrape the bowl and mix for 2 minutes. In another bowl, combine the buttermilk and apple cider syrup.

2. To the butter and egg mix, add ½ dry mix, ½ wet mix, ½ dry mix, ½ wet mix - scraping the bowl in between additions. Place the dough on floured parchment. Flour the top of the dough and gently roll out to about $^1/_3$" thick. Chill the dough in the freezer until firm enough to punch out (about 1½ hours). Punch out 2" circles of dough and place on a lightly floured tray. Punch out a 1" hole in each of the circles.

cinnamon mixture:

Mix the cinnamon and sugar together and reserve.

Calvados sabayon:

Place the eggs, yolks, sugar and ½ ounce of Calvados in bowl. Place the bowl over simmering water and whisk the mixture vigorously until it triples in volume. Remove from the heat and cool to room temperature. Whip the cream and 1 ounce Calvados to soft peaks and fold into the egg mixture. Refrigerate.

diced apples:

Combine the diced apples with the sugar and salt and add to a sauté pan. Cook on a high heat while stirring with a wooden spoon until the apples are tender and all of the juice has evaporated from the pan. Cool the apples to room temperature on a sheet tray.

to serve:

Fry the donuts in oil heated to 350°F for 1½ minutes on each side or until deep golden brown. Drain on paper towels and cool for about 2 minutes before tossing the donuts and donut holes in the cinnamon mixture. Serve with the sabayon and cooked apples.

WARM CHOCOLATE TART WITH MAPLE & HAZELNUT ICE CREAM

BY FRANCOIS BLAIS

Chiboust is one of my favorite desserts. It's light, creamy and tasty!

WARM CHOCOLATE TART WITH MAPLE & HAZELNUT ICE CREAM

BY FRANCOIS BLAIS

Serves 4

Preparation time: 45 minutes
Cooking time: 1 hour
Special equipment: Ice cream machine

ingredients

sablé Breton:

1 cup	unsalted butter
2 tsp	salt
¾ cup	sugar
6	egg yolks
2 tbsp	baking powder
2 cups	flour

chocolate chiboust:

1 cup	very good chocolate such as Valrhona (66% cocoa minimum)
7	egg whites
½ cup	sugar
7	egg yolks
1 tbsp	corn starch
¾ cup	milk
2	gelatin sheets

maple and hazelnut ice cream:

1½ cups	heavy cream
½ cup	milk
1 tbsp	milk powder
3 tbsp	toasted hazelnut powder
½ cup	dark maple syrup
6	egg yolks

to serve:

chocolate sauce

method

sablé Breton:

1. Cream the butter with the salt and sugar until a smooth texture. Add the yolks and the dry ingredients and mix to a dough. Put the dough between two sheets of parchment paper. Roll to about $\frac{1}{8}$" thick and cool in the freezer for about 30 minutes.
2. Preheat the oven to 350°F. Place the sablé dough in a removable bottom tart pan and bake for 15 minutes or until golden brown.

chocolate chiboust:

1. Melt the chocolate. Whip the egg whites with one-third of the sugar until it forms medium to firm peaks. Mix the yolks with the rest of the sugar and the corn starch. Warm the milk and slowly add it to the yolk mixture, then add the gelatin.
2. Put the mixture in a pan and back onto the stove to simmer for 1 minute. Mix half of the meringue with the warm yolk mixture. Add the melted chocolate and finish with the remaining meringue.
3. Fill the tart pan with the chocolate chiboust and let cool for 1 hour.

maple and hazelnut ice cream:

1. Heat the cream, the milk and the milk powder with the half of the maple syrup and the toasted hazelnut powder. Mix the yolks with the rest of the maple syrup. While whisking the yolks, gradually pour in the hot cream mixture. Return the mixture to cook over a low heat, stirring constantly until the custard has thickened and coats the back of a spoon.
2. Pour the mixture through a strainer and cool in the refrigerator. Freeze the ice cream in an ice cream machine then keep in the freezer.

to serve:

When you are ready to serve, cut a slice of the tart and warm in the oven for 2 minutes. Add a big spoon of ice cream and some chocolate sauce.

HUDSON VALLEY APPLE PIE

BY JEREMY MCMILLAN

AND

SAMANTHA ARDONOWSKI

The Hudson Valley grows some of the most flavorful apples I have ever eaten. On a day off the last thing I am looking for is complex, baking a pie is anything but.

HUDSON VALLEY APPLE PIE

BY JEREMY MCMILLAN AND SAMANTHA ARDONOWSKI

Serves 6

Preparation time: 1 hour
Cooking time: 45 minutes

ingredients

pie crust:

2½ cups	all purpose flour
1 tsp	salt
1 cup	unsalted butter, cut and chilled
1 cup	water

filling:

11½ lb	Granny Smith apples, peeled and sliced
3 tbsp	granulated sugar
2 tbsp	maple syrup
½ tsp	cinnamon
¼ tsp	nutmeg
3 tbsp	butter
1	vanilla bean
1 pinch	salt

method

pie crust:

Sift the flour and salt together into a mixing bowl. Rub the cold butter into the flour with your hands, pinching until the mixture resembles coarse meal. Slowly add the water and mix until it holds together. Divide the dough in half, wrap and refrigerate for at least 2 hours.

filling:

Toss the apples with the sugar, maple syrup, cinnamon & nutmeg. Over a medium heat, melt the butter and vanilla bean until the butter begins to brown. Pour over the apple mixture.

to bake:

Roll out the dough to a ¼" thickness and line a pie pan, making sure there is a 1" over hang. Pour the apple filling into the pan. Roll out the second piece of dough to a ¼" thickness and carefully lay on top of pie. Using the excess dough, crimp the edges for a tight seal. Take a paring knife and make ½" slits in the center of the pie. Bake at 350°F for 1 hour.

to serve:

Let the pie rest at room temperature until cool enough to handle, my grandmother always did this in the window of the kitchen to allow the aromas to entice us all to come inside from playing in the leaves outdoors!

STRAWBERRIES & CREAM

BY JOSEPH LENN

We have this beautiful dairy here in East Tennesse that makes wonderful buttermilk, which would remind you of crème fraîche. In the spring when we have wonderful strawberries we thought about strawberries and whipped cream, and the end result was this dish.

STRAWBERRIES & CREAM

BY JOSEPH LENN
Serves 15

Preparation time: 1½ hours
Cooking time: 1½ - 2 hours

ingredients

panna cotta:
1½ cups	half and half
¾ cup	golden cane sugar
½	vanilla bean, split and scraped
4 sheet	bronze gelatin, softened in cold water and drained
2½ cups	buttermilk, room temperature

strawberry consommé:
4 quarts	strawberries
½ cup	golden cane sugar
juice 1	lemon

pink peppercorn shortbread:
1 lb	butter
4 oz	powdered sugar
1 lb 1 oz	bread flour
1 tbsp	ground pink peppercorns

method

panna cotta:
In a small saucepan, bring to a simmer the half and half, sugar and vanilla bean. Whisk in the softened gelatin and allow this mixture to come to room temperature. Then whisk the mixture into the buttermilk. Pour into dome molds that are on a towel lined half sheet pan. Chill to set.

strawberry consommé:
Combine all the ingredients together. Cover securely with plastic wrap and place over a pan of boiling water. Make sure water does not touch the bottom of the bowl, but also make sure the water does not boil away while the consommé is working. Cook until the strawberries look tired and spent, about 1 hour. Remove from the heat and let the strawberries steep for 1 more hour off the heat. Strain without pushing through the mesh. The spent strawberries may be puréed and used for sorbet, ice cream or sauce. Chill the consommé.

pink peppercorn shortbread:
1. In a mixer with the paddle attachment, cream together the butter and powdered sugar.
2. Add the flour and peppercorns, mixing until just combined.
3. Roll the dough between 2 sheets of parchment to about ¼" thick. Chill for 1 hour, then bake for 5 minutes at 350°F Cut with the scalloped cutter that just fits in the dome molds and return the sheet pan to the oven to dry the cookies slightly. Remove from the oven and allow to cool completely before removing from the sheet pan.

to serve:
Remove the panna cotta from the mold and place it on top of the cookie. Place the cookie/panna cotta in a bowl and pour 2 ounces of the strawberry consommé. Garnish with diced strawberries and ground pink peppercorns.

BLACK PLUM UPSIDE-DOWN CAKE

BY ARNAUD COTAR

This dessert is a spur-of-the moment possibility as all ingredients are usually on hand. The plums can be interchanged with almost any firm fruit, whatever is available, such as - very ripe, fresh pineapple, raw figs, ripe peaches in season, apples and pears, which require just a bit of pre-cooking.

BLACK PLUM UPSIDE-DOWN CAKE

BY ARNAUD COTAR

Serves 8

Preparation time: 15 minutes
Cooking time: 15-20 minutes

ingredients

plums:
8	black plums
2 tbsp	unsalted butter
1 tbsp	light brown sugar

cake:
8	egg whites (large size eggs)
6	egg yolks (large size eggs)
12 oz	white sugar
12 oz	whole milk
2 tsp	vanilla extract
1 lb 1 oz	all-purpose flour
3 tsp	baking powder
3 oz	yellow cornmeal
½ tsp	baking soda
6 oz	unsalted butter

Chantilly cream:
1 cup	heavy cream
1 tsp	white sugar (or to taste)
2 drops	vanilla extract

to serve:
diced plums

CHEF'S TIP
The cake batter can be made 2 days ahead. Alternatives to the Chantilly cream are vanilla ice cream, mascarpone cheese with a bit of orange zest mixed in and white sugar to taste or, for ultimate flavor, pistachio ice cream.

method

plums:
Preheat the oven to 350°F. Halve the plums and discard the stones. Mix the butter and sugar and spoon over the plums (placed cut side up in the pan). Roast in the oven until softened but still firm, about 10 minutes.

cake:
1. Combine the egg whites, yolks and sugar in a large bowl – beat vigorously until the sugar is dissolved and the mixture is lighter in color. Mix in the milk and vanilla. Combine all the dry ingredients in a separate bowl and fold into the wet mixture. Lastly, have the butter melted and cooled down, then mix it into the batter.
2. Preheat the oven to 350°F. Butter 8 x 4 ounce ramekins and place a half plum in each, cut side up, with 1 tablespoon of roasting juices (save the remaining juices). Fill the ramekin three-quarters full with batter. Bake in the oven for 15 minutes until golden on top. Check the doneness with a clean knife and leave in the ramekins to cool.

Chantilly cream:
Beat the ingredients together until the sugar is dissolved, and peaks form.

to serve:
Turn out the ramekins onto the serving plates and drizzle with more of the roasting juices. Serve with the Chantilly cream and garnish with diced plums.

CANOE BAY'S BAKED HOT CHOCOLATE WITH MOCHA FOAM

BY JON ROSNOW

 **Growing up in Wisconsin with two older brothers made for lots of playing in the snow. The only way that my mom could get us to come in from the fun was with a big mug of creamy hot chocolate with whipped cream. I've updated this by using various chocolates and baking the dish making it one of our guests' favorites. Even better, it is a fairly easy recipe to make.**

CANOE BAY'S BAKED HOT CHOCOLATE WITH MOCHA FOAM

BY JON ROSNOW

Serves 8, 8oz servings

Preparation time: 20 minutes
Cooking time: 15 minutes
Special equipment: Cream whipper

ingredients

baked hot chocolate:

18 oz	dark chocolate
6 oz	butter, unsalted, room temperature
8 each	eggs
4 oz	sugar
pinch salt	

mocha foam:

11 oz	trimoline
1 each	egg white
¾ oz	coffee, light roast
4½ oz	cream
2 oz	white chocolate

to serve:

mint leaf
grated nutmeg

CHEF'S TIP
The batter can be prepared and poured into mugs ahead of time, so that they are ready to bake at the right moment.

method

baked hot chocolate:

1. Combine the chocolate and butter in a mixing bowl and place over a double boiler.
2. While the chocolate is melting, mix together the eggs and sugar in a mixing bowl, and warm the egg mixture to room temperature over a double boiler.
3. Once the egg mixture is warmed, use a mixer to whip the eggs until they are thick and pale yellow.
4. When the chocolate and butter are fully melted and combined, fold in the whipped eggs making sure the eggs are fully incorporated. Fold in a pinch of salt.
5. Pour the mixture into oven-safe mugs or ramekins, filling ⅔ full.
6. Place the filled mugs into a water-bath and bake at 350°F for 15 minutes. The top of the batter will bake into a cake-like crust while the bottom half remains hot chocolate.
7. Serve with mocha foam (or whipped cream), a mint leaf, and freshly grated nutmeg.

mocha foam:

1. Combine the trimoline, egg white and coffee in a mixing bowl. Whisk until incorporated and lightly airy, reserve.
2. Bring the cream to a simmer in a small saucepot. Pour the warm cream over the white chocolate and stir until the chocolate is fully melted.
3. Fold the melted chocolate into the egg white mixture and gently combine.
4. Chill the mixture before pouring into a cream whipper. Charge the cream whipper according to manufacturer's instructions.

to serve:

Serve with mocha foam (or whipped cream), a mint leaf, and freshly grated nutmeg.

TIRAMISU

BY KARSTEN HART

Tira Mi Su means 'Pick Me Up' in Italian. A dessert to raise the spirits! My wife, Deja, and I enjoy this dish served with a glass of Samuel Smith Oatmeal Stout.

TIRAMISU

BY KARSTEN HART

Serves 6

Preparation time: 1 hour
Cooking time: 30 minutes

ingredients

sabayon:

6	egg yolks
½ cup	white wine
¼ cup	Marsala
½ cup	granulated sugar
6 oz	heavy cream
1 oz	sugar, granulated
½ tsp	vanilla extractd with 1 rounded tsp cinnamon

mascarpone layer:

16 oz	mascarpone cheese
2 tbsp	coffee liquor
1 tsp	espresso powder
¼ cup	granulated sugar

to assemble:

36	small ladyfingers
½ cup	Marsala

to serve:

2 oz	dark chocolate, finely grated
1 bottle	Samuel Smith Oatmeal Stout

method

sabayon:

1. Over a double boiler, beat the egg yolks, white wine, Marsala and granulated sugar to create a sabayon. Continue to beat with a whisk for approximately 10 minutes or until the sabayon is very thick. Remove from the heat and chill over an ice bath.
2. In a separate bowl, heat the heavy cream, sugar and vanilla extract until soft peaks form. Fold into the chilled sabayon and reserve.

mascarpone layer:

In a clean bowl, combine all the ingredients. Allow the mascarpone mixture to sit at room temperature until you are ready to assemble the tiramisu.

to assemble:

Quickly dip enough of the ladyfingers in Marsala to cover the bottom of a 10" square dish. Spread half of the mascarpone mixture over the ladyfingers. Layer the sabayon mixture on top of the mascarpone and repeat. Smooth the top layer neatly and cover with plastic wrap and refrigerate for a few hours or overnight if possible to allow the flavors to develop.

to serve:

Remove the tiramisu from the refrigerator and spoon into dessert bowls or glasses. Dust with the grated chocolate and serve with Samuel Smith Oatmeal Stout. Buon Appetito!

BLACK PEPPER PANNA COTTA WITH FRESH STRAWBERRIES & SAUCE

BY ALEXANDER NAGI

This is a play on an old Italian classic that my father made me aware of when I was very young. The thought of putting freshly cracked black pepper on fresh strawberries was absurd to me, but then I tried it and I was hooked! To this day I'll try black pepper on anything, but I have yet to find a pairing as interesting as this one.

BLACK PEPPER PANNA COTTA WITH FRESH STRAWBERRIES & SAUCE

BY ALEXANDER NAGI

Serves 10

Preparation time: 20 minutes
Cooking time: 30 minutes

ingredients

panna cotta:

1 quart	heavy cream
2 tbsp	fresh ground black pepper
1 cup	sugar
7	standard sized gelatin sheets

strawberries and sauce:

1 quart	fresh strawberries, cut into ½" pieces
½ cup	sugar
1 tbsp	fresh lemon juice

method

panna cotta:

1. In a medium sized stainless steel handle pot, combine the heavy cream, crushed black pepper and sugar. Place the pot over a low heat and cook for 30 minutes, whisking occasionally. In a stainless steel mixing bowl place the 7 gelatin sheets in cold water and allow them to soften (3 minutes).
2. Carefully remove the softened gelatin sheets from the cold water and whisk them into the hot cream mixture until fully resolved. Strain the cream through a fine chinois into a jug. Pour the cream into 4x1 ounce soft plastic cups of any shape and refrigerate for at least 2 hours.

strawberries & sauce:

1. In a stainless steel mixing bowl, combine the cut strawberries and sugar and mix gently with a rubber spatula making sure to evenly coat the cut strawberries with the sugar.
2. The strawberry and sugar mixture should sit for at least a half hour to allow the strawberries to soften and create a sauce.

to serve:

Once the panna cotta is firm and ready to be plated, heat the cup in a bowl of warm water for a few seconds and carefully turn out the contents onto the center a small dessert plate. Add the lemon juice to the strawberry sauce, mix well and spoon onto the panna cotta. Garnish with some fresh ground black pepper and serve.

LEFSE

BY GUNNAR THOMPSON

This is a family recipe for special occasions.

LEFSE

BY GUNNAR THOMPSON

Serves 20-30

Preparation time:	3 hours
Cooking time:	2 hours

Special equipment:	Griddle, waxed paper or pastry cloth, potato ricer or food mill
Planning ahead:	Cook and rice the potatoes a day in advance.

ingredients

subhead:

5lb	russet potatoes, peeled and cut into quarters
¼ cup	butter, melted and cooled slightly
⅓ cup	cream
½ tbsp	salt
1 tbsp	sugar
2½ cups	flour

to serve:

¼ cup	softened sweet butter
1 cup	packed brown sugar
4	lefse

CHEF'S TIP

Scaling down the recipe does not work well, but the cooked lefse freezes exceptionally well if securely wrapped and placed in a freezer bag.

method

1. Boil the potatoes until they are fork tender. Drain well and push through a ricer or food mill. Cool overnight in the refrigerator.
2. The next day, stir in the butter, cream, salt and sugar. Work in the flour a ½ cup at a time. Let the dough relax for 30 minutes.
3. Separate a ball of dough and roll in flour to form a rope. Cut into walnut size pieces. Roll between 2 floured sheets of waxed paper.
4. Cook on a dry cast iron griddle over medium heat until browned on both sides. Cool in a light towel, stacked on top of each other. Do not try to reduce recipe size, the lefse freeze well.

to serve:

Spread the lefse with butter, sprinkle with sugar and roll up like a cigar. Cut in half and serve.

SHOOFLY PIE

BY TUCKER YODER

I have always been a huge fan of these pie/cakes with their gooey cakey filling.

SHOOFLY PIE

BY TUCKER YODER

Serves 4

Cooking time: 1 hour
Special equipment: Mini Pie Pans
Planning ahead: Have your pie crust baked off ahead of time will make this really simple

ingredients

pie dough:

1lb 2oz	all purpose flour
pinch	sugar
¾ tbsp	salt
11 oz	unsalted butter
2 tbsp	milk
2	eggs

filling:

¾ tsp	baking soda
¾ cup	boiling water
8 oz	molasses blackstrap or king syrup
1	egg
1 tsp	vanilla extract

crumb top:

5½ oz	all purpose flour
4 oz	light brown sugar
2 tbsp	unsalted butter diced
¼ tsp	kosher salt
pinch	ground cinnamon, ginger and nutmeg

CHEF'S TIP
It is a little hard to tell when these are done - just check them every 10 minutes or so should do the trick.

method

pie dough:

1. Preheat the oven to 350°F.
2. In a food processor mix the flour, sugar and salt pulsing to combine. Add the chilled diced butter, pulse to combine and make a coarse crumb that clumps when pressed in your hands. Whisk together the milk and eggs and add to the food processor and mix until a dough forms. Don't over mix.
3. Turn the dough out onto the table, wrap in plastic wrap and refrigerate for at least an hour and up to a day. Roll the dough out as thinly as possible and rest briefly after achieving the desired thickness. Cut the dough into rounds a ½" larger then your pie tins. Line the pie tins with dough pressing into corners and refrigerate for about an hour. Trim the excess dough. Line the dough with parchment and fill with raw rice or dried beans to weight it down. Bake in the oven for 10-15 minutes until cooked. Remove the parchment with beans/rice and reserve for later use.

filling:
Mix the baking soda and water. Combine the molasses, egg and vanilla and then combine the two mixtures together.

crumb top:
Combine all the ingredients in a food processor and pulse until everything is thoroughly combined.

to serve:
Pour the filling into the pre-baked pie crusts about ¼ of the way up. Top with the crumb topping to fill the pie crust. Bake at 350°F until a tooth pick comes out clean; about 20 minutes

BANANA TART WITH CREME CHANTILLY

BY MICHAEL HARRISON

This is a play on one of my all time favorite desserts, the apple tart tatin. I remember this dessert from making it at Le Gavroche restaurant in London many years ago. What I've done is use bananas which are grown locally and they work perfectly in this recipe.

BANANA TART WITH CREME CHANTILLY

BY MICHAEL HARRISON

Serves 4

Preparation time: 40 minutes
Cooking time: 25 minutes

Special equipment: Small round molds, piping bag
Planning ahead: The Chantilly cream can be made the day before.

ingredients

caramel:
8 oz	caster sugar
8 oz	water

banana tart:
4	ripe bananas
2 oz	butter diced in four
1	sheet of rolled puff pastry

crème Chantilly:
2 cups	heavy cream
3 tbsp	granulated sugar
½ pod	vanilla pod
1 tsp	vanilla extract

method

caramel:
Place the ingredients in a pot and boil until golden brown, spoon ¾ of it into 4 molds

banana tart:
In each mold, slice 1 banana and place ½ ounce of butter in each. Cut the puff pastry into circles to fit over the mold and place over the bananas and butter, making a few holes with a fork. Bake for 25 minutes at 350ºF.

crème Chantilly:
In a large mixing bowl, beat the heavy cream, sugar, vanilla pod and extract together on high speed until soft peaks form in the mixture.

to serve:
Place the tart in middle of the plate, pipe some crème Chantilly using a piping bag and garnish with a slice of strawberry and caramel.

SQUASH PANNA COTTA

BY THOMAS CROIZE

**This light yet earthy panna cotta is a wonderful alternative to a traditional Thanksgiving pumpkin pie for a holiday dessert. I added a cranberry compote for its tartness and an almond tuile for a satisfying crunch.**

SQUASH PANNA COTTA

BY THOMAS CROIZE

Serves 8

Preparation time: 1 day
Cooking time: 2½ hours

Special equipment: 8" x ½" diameter dome silicone baking molds or 8 ramekins
Planning ahead: The day before make the panna cotta and almond tuile batter

ingredients

panna cotta:

3 cups	milk
4	¼" thick slices peeled ginger
1 strip	orange zest, removed with a vegetable peeler
2 points	star anise
1	vanilla bean, split lengthwise and scraped, pulp reserved
1	3" cinnamon stick
¼ tsp	salt
1¾ lbs	kabocha squash, peeled, seeded and cut into 1" chunks
6 tbsp	sugar
1¼-2 cups	heavy cream
1 packet	unflavored gelatin

almond tuile:

3 tbsp	unsalted butter, melted and cooled
1 tbsp	light corn syrup
¼ cup	sugar
½ cup	sliced blanched almonds

pumpkin sauce:

1 tbsp	sugar
1½ tsp	apple pectin
1 cup	pumpkin purée
1 pinch	cinnamon

cranberry compote:

3 cups	fresh or frozen cranberries
¾ cup	sugar
¾ cup	water
2	¼" thick slices peeled ginger
½	vanilla bean, split lengthwise and scraped, pulp reserved
½	3" cinnamon stick
1 pinch	salt

method

panna cotta:

1. Combine the milk, ginger, orange zest, star anise, vanilla bean pod and pulp, cinnamon, and salt in a medium saucepan and bring to a simmer. Remove from the heat, cover and allow to infuse for 20 minutes.
2. Strain the milk through a sieve set over a bowl. Return to the same saucepan and add the squash. Bring to a boil, reduce the heat to a simmer and poach until the squash is very tender, about 20 minutes. Add the sugar, stir until dissolved and remove from the heat.
3. Transfer the squash mixture to a blender or food processor and purée until smooth. Strain through a fine-mesh sieve into a 4-cup liquid measure; discard the solids. Add enough cream to equal 3½ cups and stir to combine.
4. Sprinkle the gelatin over 2 tablespoons water in a small saucepan; stand for 5 minutes to soften. Add a ½ cup of the squash purée to the gelatin. Warm over a low heat, stirring until the gelatin dissolves. Stir into the remaining squash mixture.
5. Divide the panna cotta mixture among 8" x 3½" diameter silicon baking molds or ramekins. Refrigerate overnight.

almond tuile:

1. Whisk together the butter, corn syrup, sugar and almonds in a small bowl. Cover with plastic wrap, pressing the plastic directly against the surface of the batter. Refrigerate for at least 2 hours or overnight. Center a rack in the oven and preheat the oven to 350°F.
2. For each tuile, drop a ½ teaspoon of the batter onto a non-stick baking sheet, leaving 2" between each drop of batter.

Press the batter lightly with your thumb until each drop is about 1" in diameter. Bake for 8-10 minutes until the tuiles are thin, lacy and golden brown. Remove from the oven, wait 1 minute and then using a plastic spatula, remove the tuiles from the baking sheet; cool over top of a rolling pin to make a curved shape. Store in an airtight container in a cool, dry environment.

pumpkin sauce:

In a small bowl, combine the sugar and apple pectin. In a medium saucepan, combine the purée and cinnamon and bring to a simmer. Whisk in the sugar mixture and cook, whisking constantly for 3 minutes. Transfer to a bowl, cover and chill.

compote:

1. Combine all the ingredients in a small saucepan; cook over a medium heat, stirring until the cranberries start to lose their shape and most of the liquid has evaporated, 10-15 minutes.
2. Remove from the heat, scrape the compote onto a plate and press a piece of plastic wrap against the surface of the compote. Refrigerate for at least 1 hour. Before serving, discard the ginger, vanilla-bean pod and cinnamon stick. Serve chilled or at room temperature.

to serve:

To un-mold, run the tip of a small knife around the edges of the panna cottas. Dip the ramekins halfway into a bowl of hot water for 5-10 seconds. Dry the bottom of each mold and invert each one onto a dessert plate. Tap lightly to release them. Garnish with a spoonful of cranberry compote, an almond tuile and a few spoonfuls of pumpkin sauce.

SPEZZATA DI CASTAGNE WITH ZESTED MASCARPONE

BY BROOKS HEADLEY

This is a fine dessert to bust out at home when you are feeling a little bit lazy. It's easy, and you can even be several glasses of Krug in, and I swear it will still come out so great. It has chestnuts done Italian style, but fresh and light and delicious. The unmelted turbinado sugar on top is key. It's there for crunch and for a textural reward. Make it at your beach house for Christmas and I guarantee your friends and family will be love it!

SPEZZATA DI CASTAGNE WITH ZESTED MASCARPONE

BY BROOKS HEADLEY

Serves 5

Preparation time: 15 minutes
Cooking time: 15-20 minutes or until tender

ingredients

steamed chestnuts:

1lb	fresh chestnuts, steamed or boiled in their shells
	salt & pepper, to taste
1-1½ tbsp	extra-virgin olive oil
zest of 2	tangerines
2 shakes	white wine vinegar

zested mascarpone:

1lb	good mascarpone cheese
2 tbsp	turbinado sugar, plus more for garnish
zest of 3	Meyer lemons
zest of 3	tangerines
1 pinch	salt

method

steamed chestnuts:

Cut the chestnuts in half while still warm and then remove the meat. Tear the chestnut meat into large pieces and season with salt and pepper to taste. Dress lightly with olive oil, the tangerine zest and the vinegar. Toss to combine.

zested mascarpone:

Combine all the ingredients and fluff together with a fork, without dissolving the sugar.

to serve:

Spoon 2 tablespoons of the zested mascarpone on a plate. Top with a mound of the seasoned chestnuts. Sprinkle a few more grains of sugar over the top and serve immediately.

Chefs at Home: *Desserts*

LITCHI & PINK GRAPEFRUIT TEMPTATION

BY JEAN-CLAUDE DUFOUR

 Best enjoyed with a glass of pink Champagne, this tantalizing dessert with fresh fruity flavors is the perfect ending to any meal and can be served with a scoop of homemade ice cream.

LITCHI & PINK GRAPEFRUIT TEMPTATION

BY JEAN-CLAUDE DUFOUR

Serves 8

Preparation time: 1 hours 20 minutes
Cooking time: 20 minutes

ingredients

pastry:

5 oz	soft butter
5 oz	icing sugar
1 tsp	salt
10 oz	flour
2	eggs

litchi ganache:

3½ oz	litchi juice
10 oz	white chocolate
1½ oz	white chocolate for the pie bottom
2	sheets of gelatin, bloomed (softened in cold water)
3½ oz	liquid cream

grapefruit cream:

4½ oz	Chinese grapefruit juice
4	eggs
8	egg yolks
7 oz	caster sugar
8½ oz	butter
2	sheets of gelatin, bloomed

pink icing:

3 oz	water
4½ oz	caster sugar
2	sheets of gelatin, bloomed
	red food coloring
2	sheets of gelatin, bloomed

to serve:

homemade ice cream

CHEF'S TIP
Crystallized rose petals or a thin layer of white chocolate may be used to decorate the tart.

method

pastry:

1. Mix the butter and sugar to form a smooth paste. Add the salt, flour and eggs, mixing until the pastry can be shaped into a ball. Place the pastry, covered in plastic, in the fridge for approximately 20 minutes.
2. Roll into a circle large enough to cover a buttered pie form. Return the pie dish to the fridge and leave for 1 hour. Preheat the oven to 400°F. Dock the dough with a fork. Bake in the oven for approximately 20 minutes, until cooked.

litchi ganache:

1. Melt the 10 ounces of white chocolate. Mix the litchi juice and cream together and bring to a quick boil. Mix with the white chocolate and add the softened gelatin. Mix together into a homogeneous cream.
2. Melt the white chocolate and spread onto the pie bottom. Cover the chocolate base with the litchi ganache.

grapefruit cream:

Bring the juice to a quick boil. Whisk the eggs, yolks and sugar together until the sugar is dissolved. Continue to beat the mixture over a bain marie until cooked. Whisk in the butter and add the softened gelatin. Place in the fridge to cool down, then pour on top of the ganache and fill the pie dish nearly up to the top.

pink icing:

1. Boil the water and sugar for 5 minutes until it becomes syrupy (220°F with a sugar thermometer). Pour the syrup onto the softened gelatin and add a few drops of the red food coloring until the icing becomes a light pink color.
2. Leave the icing to cool down to room temperature (to avoid melting the grapefruit cream, the icing must be cooled down sufficiently). The icing will thicken slightly, making it ideal to cover the pie.

to serve:

Serve with a scoop of homemade ice cream.

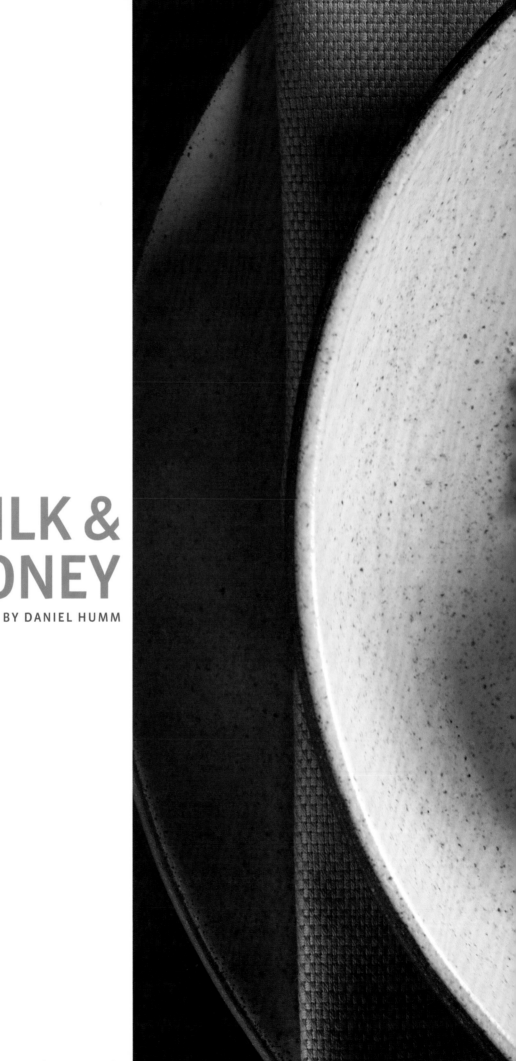

MILK &
HONEY

BY DANIEL HUMM

Growing up, my mom would give me a glass of warm milk with a spoonful of honey before going to bed. So many years later, it's still one of my fondest food memories, and, as such, I've always wanted to make a dessert that brought to life that memory. In combining the milk in various textures-dehydrated and as a sorbet -with smooth, floral, sweet honey, I longed to make a dessert that was at once modern and familiar, recognizable and new.

MILK & HONEY

BY DANIEL HUMM

Serves 4

Preparation time: 2 hours for the ice milk
Cooking time: up to 12 hours for milk foam

ingredients

milk ice:
3¼ cups   milk
½ cup + 1 tbsp cream
½ cup + 1 tbsp powdered milk
⅓ cup   sugar
2 tbsp   glucose syrup
1 tsp   salt

honey oatmeal crumble:
1½ cup + 2 tbsp butter, softened
⅓ cup   sugar
¼ cup   honey
1 tsp   salt
½ tsp   vanilla extract
1 cup + 1 tbsp flour
½ cup   old-fashioned rolled oats
¼ tsp   baking soda

honey brittle:
1 cup   sugar
¼ cup   butter
2 tbsp   honey
1½ tsp   salt
½ tsp   baking soda

dehydrated milk foam:
2 cups   milk
5 tbsp   glucose syrup

to serve:
buckwheat honey

method

milk ice:
In a small saucepan on a medium-high heat, reduce 2 cups of the milk to ⅔ cup. Combine the reduced milk with the remaining ingredients in a blender and blend until smooth. Strain through a chinois then chill over ice. Freeze the mixture in an ice cream machine according to manufacturer's instructions. Store in the freezer for up to 1 month.

honey oatmeal crumble:
Preheat the oven to 300°F. In a stand mixer fitted with the paddle attachment, cream together the butter, sugar, honey, salt, and vanilla. Add the flour, oats, and baking soda, mixing until just combined. Turn the dough out onto a piece of parchment paper and roll to ¼" thick. Transfer to a rimmed baking sheet and bake until golden brown, about 15 minutes. Lower the oven temperature to 150°F and continue to dry for 30 minutes, checking the dough to make sure it does not get too dark. Cool at room temperature before storing in an airtight container.

honey brittle:
Line a 13"x18" rimmed baking sheet with parchment paper. In a medium straight-sided sauté pan bring the sugar, butter, honey, and ¼ cup water to a boil. Cook over a medium high heat until it is a light caramel, about 2 minutes. Add the salt and baking soda and mix well. Pour the brittle in a thin layer onto the baking sheet. Allow to cool completely at room temperature before breaking into small pieces.

dehydrated milk foam:
Preheat the oven to 150°F. Line a 9"x13" rimmed baking sheet with acetate. In a medium saucepan, heat the milk and glucose to just under a boil. Remove from the heat and froth with a hand blender. Scoop the foam out with a large spoon onto the prepared baking sheet, discarding any liquid. Dry in the oven overnight, 8-9 hours. Allow the foam to cool before breaking it into small pieces. Store in an airtight container.

to serve:
Place a small amount of the dehydrated milk foam, honey brittle, and honey oatmeal crumble in a small bowl. Spoon a large quenelle of milk ice on top. Drizzle lines of buckwheat honey across the top of the quenelle.

MEXICAN RICE PUDDING WITH CARAMEL SAUCE

BY GONZALO CERDA

Rice pudding is one of the most traditional preparations in Mexico, one of the most humble and simple desserts, but at the same time so complex for its texture that makes it so interesting and one of my favorites.

MEXICAN RICE PUDDING WITH CARAMEL SAUCE

BY GONZALO CERDA

Serves 4

Preparation time: 30 minutes
Cooking time: 45 minutes

ingredients

rice pudding:

1 cup	long grain rice
1	cinnamon stick
Peel 1	orange
50 oz	whole milk
3½ oz	raisins
2 cans (28 oz) condensed milk	
cinnamon dust for garnish	

caramel sauce:

5 oz	sugar
17 oz	milk
¾ oz	unsalted butter

method

rice pudding:

1. Rinse the rice in cold water and drain several times until the water stops coming out cloudy. Put it in a pot and add water until it covers the rice, simmer with cinnamon and orange peel until all the water evaporates.
2. Add the milk and continue simmering until the rice is al dente. Add the raisins and condensed milk until dissolved.

caramel sauce:

Put the sugar into a pan on a low heat until it caramelizes. Once caramelized, slowly add the milk until completely incorporated and then add the butter to the sauce until dissolved and mixed in. Allow to cool.

to serve:

Once the rice is cooled, serve in a bowl, sprinkle with a dusting of cinnamon and pour over the sauce.

MEXICAN CHURROS

BY ALEXIS PALACIOS

These miniature vanilla churros with Cajeta caramel are so delicious you'll keep coming back for more!

MEXICAN CHURROS

BY ALEXIS PALACIOS

Serves 4

Preparation time: 25 minutes
Cooking time: 5-8 minutes

ingredients

churros dough:

1¾ pt	water
1 oz	salt
10 oz	butter
1 lb	flour
10	eggs
vegetable oil, for frying	
2 oz	sugar mixed with cinnamon

Cajeta caramel:

6 oz	sugar
10 oz	milk

CHEF'S TIP
Use your favorite ice cream to serve with the churros.

method

churros dough:

1. Boil the water with the salt and butter, add the flour and cook for 15 minutes over a slow heat, working the dough all the time, then allow it to cool down. Put the dough in a mixer and add the eggs one by one. Beat the dough for 10 minutes.
2. Put the dough in a piping bag, and pipe into churros shapes. Fry them in the oil for approximately 5-8 minutes. Remove and dust with sugar and cinnamon.

Cajeta caramel:

Heat the sugar until it starts to dissolve into a caramel, then add the milk little by little and mix it in. Reduce the mixture to half.

to serve:

Placed the churros on a plate and use the Cajeta caramel as a dipping sauce.

GOLDEN STAR APPLE BEIGNET, ROSE HIP COULIS, FROMAGE BLANC GLACE

BY JEAN JOHO

This recipe is a new interpretation of a classic apple beignet. I have a great farmer in Michigan who grows heirloom apples. Rose hips are extremely popular in Alsace.

GOLDEN STAR APPLE BEIGNET, ROSE HIP COULIS, FROMAGE BLANC GLACE

BY JEAN JOHO

Serves 4

Preparation time: 1 hour
Cooking time: 10 minutes

Planning ahead: The batter needs to be mixed the night before.
Special equipment: Thermometer

ingredients

beer batter:

2 cups	all purpose flour
1	pinch of salt
1	pinch of sugar
2	egg yolks
10 oz	beer
1 tsp	canola oil

golden star apple beignet:

frying oil
4   golden star apples
sugar, to taste
Alsace kirsch eau de vie, to taste
3   egg whites
cinnamon sugar

to serve:

rose hip coulis
kirsch and cheese ice cream

method

beer batter:

Mix all the ingredients together and set aside overnight.

golden star apple beignet:

1. Preheat the frying oil to 375°F on a thermometer. Peel and core the apples and cut with a small knife into a spiral. Sprinkle with a touch of sugar and the kirsch.
2. Whip the egg whites to soft peaks and fold into the batter. Coat each apple in batter and fry until golden brown. Set on paper towels to drain. Sprinkle with cinnamon sugar.

to serve:

Garnish a serving platter with the rose hip coulis.
Place a beignet on top and serve with the ice cream.

CHEF'S TIP
You can substitute the golden star apples with any other crisp apples.

TREACLE TART WITH LEMON CURD & MILK JAM

BY COLIN BEDFORD

This is a dish that I had when I was a child and was a classic that featured in a good old English pub.

Preparation time: 90 minutes
It is paramount to rest the pastry. Prep time can be longer as fridge resting is require and allowing components overnight in the fridge will improve flavor.

Cooking time: 4 hours
This looks worse than it actually is, watching a can of condensed milk boiling for 3 hours and then the tart takes about an hour to cook.

Special equipment:
Silpat is a good idea when make the tuiles and meringue drops to limit sticking and breakage.

Planning ahead:
The bread crumbs in the food processor with work better I you use day old bread which has been left out. Making the tuile batter the day before is key.

ingredients

treacle tart dough:

14 oz	bread flour
10 oz	butter
3½ oz	powdered sugar
1 tsp	salt
1	lemon
1 tsp	vanilla
2	whole eggs

tart filling:

3 oz	brown bread crumbs
1#	golden syrup
3½ oz	butter
3 oz	whole eggs
5 tbsp	cream
1 tsp	salt
2	lemon zest
1	lemon juice

lemon curd:

6 oz	butter
5 oz	egg yolks
6 oz	whole eggs
1 cup	lemon juice
6 oz	sugar

apple chutney:

2	Granny Smith apples
⅓ cup	granulated sugar
⅓ cup	white wine
⅓ cup	white wine vinegar
½	vanilla bean

whole wheat tuile:

2 oz	melted butter
3 oz	powdered sugar
1 oz	honey
2	egg whites
3 oz	whole wheat flour
pinch	ground ginger

meringue drops:

4	egg whites
4 oz	sugar
4 oz	powdered sugar

cinnamon crunch:

2 tbsp	vegetable oil
1 cup	panko breadcrumbs
1 tbsp	butter
2 tbsp	light brown sugar
½ tsp	salt
¼ tsp	cinnamon

milk jam:

14 oz can	condensed milk

to serve:
white chocolate shavings

TREACLE TART WITH LEMON CURD & MILK JAM

BY COLIN BEDFORD

Serves 6

method

tart dough:

1. To make the pastry, place the flour and butter in a food processor. Pulse until the flour has a sandy texture, then add the remaining ingredients adding the eggs last. Pulse until the dough comes together, then wrap and refrigerate for a few hours. Line a 12" by 6" rectangle pan.

2. Blind bake with baking beans on 325°F for 30 minutes until the pastry has dried out, then paint with an egg yolk to seal the pastry.

treacle tart mix:

Make sure the crusts are cut off the bread and then run through the food processor. Pre-heat oven to 300°F. Combine the golden syrup and melted butter and warm to make a liquid consistency. Whisk together the eggs, cream and salt and once fully incorporated combine with the syrup mixture. Fold in the breadcrumbs, zest and juice. Pour into a pastry case and bake until golden brown, this takes about 60 minutes.

lemon curd:

Cut the butter into small pieces and place in the fridge. Combine all the other ingredients in a non-stick sauce pan. Place on the stove on a medium - low heat and continue to whisk non-stop until it begins to boil. As soon as one bubble appears remove from the heat, whisk in the cold butter and chill.

apple chutney:

Dice the apples into $\frac{1}{8}$" dice and reserve in lemon water. Combine all the remaining ingredients, add to a pan and reduce on a high heat. Once reduced by half, add the apples and continue until the apples look translucent. Reduce as quickly as possible, to not over cook apples. Then cool.

whole wheat tuile batter:

Melt the butter and reserve. Combine all the other ingredients and make a smooth paste. Then slowly add the melted butter until fully incorporated and chill. Cut a template out of plastic 1"x10". Lay the template on silpat and spread the batter and then bake at 350°F until it turns golden brown. While hot, form around a cylinder to where the ends just overlap and place in an air tight container.

meringue drops:

Whisk the whites to soft peaks then gradually add the granulated sugar whisking for 5 minutes. Fold in the powered sugar and pipe on to the silpat in tear drop shapes. Then bake on as low a heat as possible for about 30–35 minutes until you are able to remove them in one piece.

cinnamon crunch:

Heat 2 tablespoons of vegetable oil in a frying pan on a medium-high heat and add the breadcrumbs. Toast in the pan until they begin to turn a light brown. Then add the butter, sugar and salt and continue until golden brown. Whilst hot, add the cinnamon, mix and chill.

milk jam:

Boil an elevated can from the bottom of the pan of condensed milk for 4 hours and chill.

to serve:

1. Cut the tart into rectangles and put the lemon curd into a piping bag or squeeze bottle, leaving the milk jam in the fridge as long as possible.

2. Place the tart on the plate, next to it put a small dot of lemon curd which will act as glue to hold the tuile. Drop the apple chutney across the plate and some on the tart, repeat with the cinnamon crunch. Fill in any areas with dots of lemon curd and place the meringue drops in the plate. Shave white chocolate across the plate with a microplane, then taking a warm spoonful of milk jam, direct it to the tuile and using the back of another warm spoon remove the jam forming a random shape.

ROAST CARAMEL PEARS WITH GINGERBREAD, NUTMEG ICE CREAM TRUFFLES

BY GARY DANKO

This dish is a classic combination of American flavors: warm caramel roasted pears and spiced gingerbread served alongside a nutmeg flavored ice cream truffle – a play on warm and cool. Although there are three components to this dish you may serve it simply as caramel pears on a slice of gingerbread, either with whipped cream or vanilla ice cream.

ROAST CARAMEL PEARS WITH GINGERBREAD, NUTMEG ICE CREAM TRUFFLES

BY GARY DANKO

Serves 6

Preparation time: The three separate components take 25 minutes each
Cooking time: 1 hour 20 minutes

Special equipment: Ice cream machine
Planning ahead: The nutmeg ice cream can be made in advance

ingredients

roast caramel pears:

6	large Bartlett pears, perfectly ripe
¾ cup	brown sugar
½ cup	apple cider, as needed

gingerbread:

2 cups	all purpose flour
2 tsp	baking soda
1 tsp	ground cloves
1 tsp	ground ginger
½ tsp	nutmeg, grated
¾ tsp	salt
3	large eggs
1 cup	sugar
1 cup	molasses
½ cup	corn oil
1 cup	boiling water

nutmeg ice cream truffles:

1½ cups	heavy cream
1½ cups	milk
½	vanilla bean, split
½ tsp	nutmeg, grated
¼ tsp	salt
10	egg yolks
1 cup + 3 tbsp	sugar
1½ cups	heavy cream

garnish:
mint

method

roast caramel pears:

1. Preheat the oven to 350°F. On a 12½" x 16½" sturdy aluminum sheet pan spread the brown sugar. Peel, halve and core the pears. Lay the cut side down onto the brown sugar. The pears should snugly fit into the pan. Bake in the oven until the pears are tender and their juices have formed a light caramel syrup.
   If the pan is dry add a little apple cider to help dissolve the sugar. Turn the pears over and bake for 5-10 more minutes. The results should be golden pears with a nice caramel syrup. Cool. They may be served like this or molded.

2. To mold the caramel pears, in a 4-5 ounce ramekin or mold arrange two halves of pears. Press firmly on them to compress and take on the shape of the mold. Place a round of gingerbread on top of the pears. Wrap each mold in plastic wrap. Reserve the syrup.

gingerbread:

1. Preheat the oven to 350°F. In a large bowl combine the flour, baking soda, cloves, ginger, nutmeg and salt. In a separate bowl combine the eggs, sugar, molasses, oil and boiling water. Stir the liquids into the dry ingredients. Pour into a 9" cake pan with a bottom that has been lined with parchment paper. Bake in the oven until a skewer comes out clean, about 35-45 minutes. Cool. Cut in half horizontally into ½" thickness. Cut into 6"x 3" rounds or large enough to just fill the top of ramekins.

2. Preheat the oven to 300°F. Place all the scraps and trimmings from the gingerbread on a sheet pan and place in the oven. Bake for 20 minutes or until they are dry. You may also let them air dry and finish in a warm oven. They should be completely dry. In a food processor grind into fine crumbs. Store covered until needed.

nutmeg ice cream truffles:

1. In a saucepan combine 1½ cups of cream, milk, vanilla bean, nutmeg and salt. Place over a medium heat and bring to just under a boil.

2. Meanwhile in a thick-bottomed non-reactive saucepan combine the egg yolks and sugar. Gradually whisk the hot cream into the egg yolk-sugar mixture. Cook over a medium heat, stirring constantly, until the mixture starts to thicken and lightly coats the back of a spoon. Do not allow the mixture to boil. Add the remaining 1½ cups of cream. Strain and cool completely, overnight if desired. Freeze in an ice cream machine of choice. Store in the freezer until needed.

3. To make the truffles form the ice cream into 1½" balls and roll in the crumbs. Hold the 'truffles' in the freezer until serving time.

to serve:

1. Preheat the oven to 325°F. Place individual plastic wrapped molded pears on a sheet pan in the oven.

2. Let them warm for 25-30 minutes. Once they are heated through hold until serving time. Remove the plastic and invert the molded pear onto a plate. Warm the reserved syrup and spoon a tablespoon over the pear, and arrange a frozen 'truffle' alongside. Garnish with mint and serve.

93

Chefs at Home: *Desserts*

MANGO SOUFFLE, COCO NIBS & STRAWBERRY SORBET

BY JOE SCHAFER

A timeless classic that people enjoy. We do innumerable combinations of soufflé and ice cream, usually what is seasonal and fresh.

MANGO SOUFFLE, COCO NIBS & STRAWBERRY SORBET

BY JOE SCHAFER

Serves 4

Preparation time: 14 minutes
Cooking time: 30 minutes + freezing time for sorbet

Planning ahead: The sorbet must be made the day before and frozen for 24 hours.
Special equipment: Pacojet

ingredients

sorbet:

1 lb	strawberry purée or fresh strawberries
3 oz	sugar
1½ oz	glucose
7 fl oz	water
½ fl oz	vodka

soufflé base:

2 lb 4 oz	mango purée
3½ oz	sugar
1	pinch of cornstarch
few drops of citric acid	

soufflé:

3½ oz	soufflé base (see recipe above)
2½ oz	sugar + extra to coat the ramekins
3 oz	egg whites
butter	

garnish:
coco nibs

method

sorbet:
Bring the strawberry purée/strawberries, sugar, glucose and water to a boil. Let cool to room temperature and add the vodka. Place in a Pacojet beaker and freeze for 24 hours. Spin when needed.

soufflé base:
Add the citric acid to the purée and reduce the purée by $^2/_3$. Wet the sugar and cook to a softball stage at 238°F. Add to the reduced purée and add the cornstarch. Bring to a boil and let the mixture fully thicken. Cool in a refrigerator.

soufflé:
Preheat the oven to 350°F. With a pastry brush and very soft butter brush the inside of four ramekins. Coat completely with sugar and refrigerate. Bring the egg whites to room temperature and whip in a mixer on a low speed. Slowly add the sugar and let whip for 10 minutes. Gently fold the egg whites into the soufflé base by hand with a rubber spatula. Overfill the ramekins with the mixture and level with the back of a knife. Bake in the oven for 14 minutes.

to serve:
Garnish the soufflé with coco nibs and serve with the sorbet.

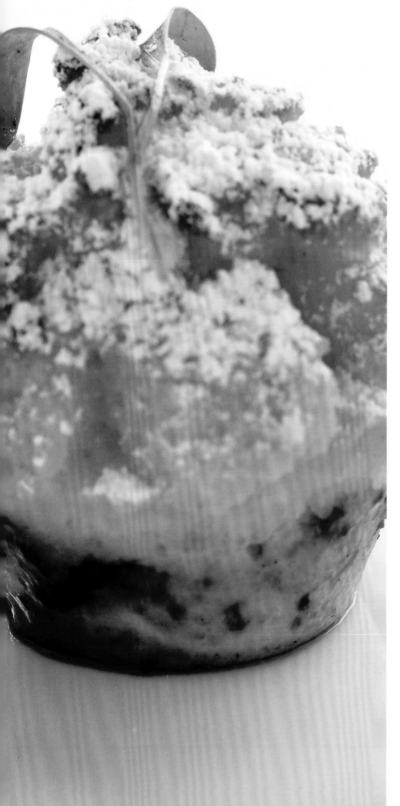

CONCORD GRAPE BREAD PUDDING

BY TAIESHA MARTIN

When I was a kid one of my all time favorite things to have for breakfast was buttered toast with grape jelly which is what the inspiration was behind this dessert.

CONCORD GRAPE BREAD PUDDING

BY TAIESHA MARTIN

Serves 8

Preparation time: 35 minutes
Cooking time: 20-25 minutes

ingredients

concord grape jelly:

1 pint	concord grapes
1½ cups	granulated sugar
¼ cup	water
½	cinnamon stick
1 tsp	apple pectin powder

bread pudding:

1 cup	granulated sugar
1 pinch	salt
2 cups	eggs
2 tbsp	vanilla extract
3 cups	whole milk
1 cup	heavy cream
½ cup	sour cream
zest of 1	lemon
1 half	brioche, cubed with crust removed

CHEF'S TIP

This dessert goes well with a nice lemon sorbet and cilantro to garnish.

method

concord grape jelly:

Combine all the ingredients in a large pot over a medium heat. Bring to a boil, and stir for 2 minutes at a rolling boil. Remove from the heat then pass the jelly through a fine mesh sieve or strainer into a bowl. Allow to cool in the refrigerator.

bread pudding:

1. Preheat the oven to 325°F and prepare one 24 cup mini muffin pan with non-stick cooking spray.
2. With a whisk combine the sugar, salt and whole eggs. Heat all the liquids and temper them over the egg mixture, then with a mesh sieve strain the batter onto the bread and set aside. Using a slotted spoon drain out a tablespoon of the bread pudding at a time and place it into the prepared muffin pans, filling it only halfway up the sides. Next, with a small spoon or piping bag, place about 1½ teaspoons of the concord grape jelly in the middle of each bread pudding. Lastly top each muffin mold off with the remainder of the drained bread pudding, mounding it on to create a cap.
3. Create a water bath in the oven by placing the bread pudding on top of a sheet pan, then filling it with water less than halfway up the sides. Bake in the oven for 20-25 minutes or until a light golden brown. Drain out the water bath and let cool at room temperature, then gently remove from the molds using a butter knife or small spoon.

to serve:

Before your guests arrival place the puddings back in the oven for 5 minutes and serve warm.

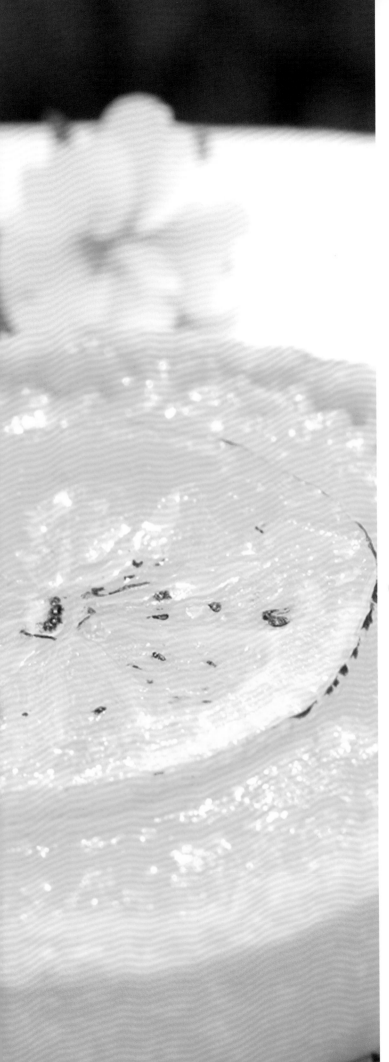

SWEET LEMON TART

BY MARCEL KAUER

We serve this sweet yet slightly tart pastry for afternoon tea or as a lovely dessert. The dough for this recipe should be made several hours or even a day before baking.

SWEET LEMON TART

BY MARCEL KAUER

Serves 4

Cooking time: 20-25 minutes
Planning ahead: Make the dough for the tart shell the day before and chill overnight.

ingredients

tart shell:

1 cup	all-purpose flour
2 tbsp	sugar
½ tsp	lemon or orange zest
¼ cup	butter
1	egg yolk
1 tbsp	ice cold water

lemon filling:

2	eggs
²/₃ cup	sugar
¹/₃ cup	lemon juice
4 tsp	melted salted butter
2 tsp	lemon zest

method

tart shell:

1. In a mixer fitted with a paddle attachment, mix the flour, sugar and zest for 1 minute. Add the butter and mix just until crumbly/sandy in texture. In a separate bowl, whisk the egg yolk and cold water together. With the mixer at medium speed, slowly add the egg and water until a dough forms. Wrap in plastic and chill for several hours or overnight. Let the dough soften slightly at room temperature before rolling.
2. Preheat the oven to 350°F. Roll the dough out on a lightly floured surface into a 10" circle. Roll it onto the pin and lay inside a lightly greased and floured tart pan with removable bottom. Press the dough into the edges of the pan and trim off excess by pressing the rolling pin around the rim. Put the tart pan on a baking sheet and prick the bottom of the dough with a fork. Cover the shell with parchment paper and fill with weights or dry beans to maintain shape and bake for 20-25 minutes.

lemon filling:

1. Whisk together the eggs, sugar, lemon juice, butter and lemon zest until smooth. Slowly pour the filling into the shell.
2. Transfer to the oven and bake the tart until the filling is barely set. Check the tart after 20 minutes and keep checking every few minutes to ensure the filling does not overcook. Cool to room temperature.

to serve:

Top with a very thin slice of fresh lemon and serve with berries and lightly sweetened whipped cream. Makes one large tart or 4 small tarts.

WARM PALISADE PEACH & BLACKBERRY COBBLER

BY CLYDE NELSON

At the ranch our guiding principle is 'always fresh from scratch'. Our cobbler is served warm right out of the oven. Palisade peaches are grown at high altitude in the intense summer sun. They're the sweetest we've ever had.

WARM PALISADE PEACH & BLACKBERRY COBBLER

BY CLYDE NELSON

Serves 4-6

Preparation time: 30 minutes
Cooking time: 20-45 minutes

ingredients

cobbler batter:

1 cup	all purpose flour
¾ tsp	baking powder
⅛ tsp	salt
¾ cup	granulated sugar
8 oz	unsalted butter, at room temperature
2	large eggs, at room temperature
1 tsp	vanilla extract

filling:

4-6	large ripe peaches
1-2 cups	blackberries
¾ cup	sugar
⅓ cup	flour
1 tbsp	cinnamon
2 oz	Bourbon whiskey

method

cobbler batter:

Sift together the flour, baking powder and salt; set aside. Cream together for several minutes the butter and sugar until light and fluffy. Add the eggs and vanilla and continue to mix until incorporated. Add the dry ingredients in batches to the butter mixture. Mix with a wooden spoon until just smooth. Set aside.

filling:

1. Preheat the oven to 350°F. Lightly butter six 8 ounce ramekins or one 2 quart casserole dish.
2. Bring one 2 quart pot of water to a boil. Score an 'X' on the peach skin on the non-stem end. Plunge the peaches into boiling water for 30 seconds. Remove and plunge the peaches into ice water. Drain. Peel away the skin. Slice the peaches into ¼" sections. Toss together the sliced peaches and blackberries with the sugar, flour and cinnamon in a mixing bowl. Add the Bourbon. Spoon the filling into the ramekins or baking dish and top with the batter, spreading it evenly to cover. Bake the ramekins for 20-25 minutes or for the casserole dish 30-45 minutes or until browned, the cake set and the fruit bubbly. Let cool slightly before serving.

to serve:

Serve the cobbler hot from the oven with ice cream.

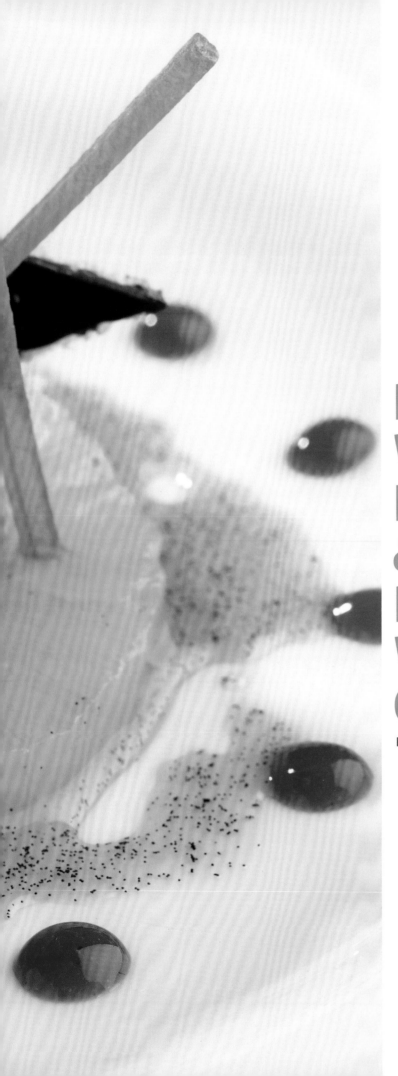

RICE PUDDING WITH GOLDEN PINEAPPLE & CRISPED RICE DIAMONDS WITH CHOCOLATE

BY THOMAS HENKELMANN

**This recipe says home, hearth and comfort. It's a treat to let your family know just how special they are to you.**

RICE PUDDING WITH GOLDEN PINEAPPLE & CRISPED RICE DIAMONDS WITH CHOCOLATE

BY THOMAS HENKELMANN

Serves 6

Preparation time: 1 hour
Cooking time: 45 minutes

ingredients

rice pudding:

4 ½ oz	long grain rice
1 quart	milk
4 oz	sugar
1 oz	diced candied orange peel
1 oz	diced candied lemon peel
2	Bourbon vanilla beans
4	sheet gelatin
½ quart	whipped cream

pineapple:

2	Bourbon vanilla beans, split in half and scraped out
1	lemon cut in half
5 oz	granulated sugar
1 cup	dry white wine
3 cups	water
1	golden pineapple, peeled and cored and cut in 12-14 even slices

crisped rice diamonds with chocolate:

8 oz	premium unsalted butter
10 oz	marshmallows
6 cups	rice cereal
¾ lb	chocolate, melted

CHEF'S TIP
Can also be served with fresh fruits or mixed berries.

method

rice pudding:

1. Wash the rice in a large volume of water, changing the water frequently until it is clear.
2. In a non reactive saucepan, place the rice, milk, 2 ounces of sugar, candied orange and lemon peel. Cut the vanilla beans length wise and scrape the pod off with the back of knife. Add the pod and bean to the pot, bring all to a boil and let simmer until the milk is almost all evaporated. Check if the rice is tender, add extra milk if needed and cook until the rice is cooked.
3. Soak the gelatin sheets in cold water and when soft, remove from the water and press any extra water out. Add to the hot rice, mix and remove the vanilla beans. Let the rice cool down in a mixing bowl. Meanwhile whip the cream and remaining sugar until semi firm peaks are reached. Gently blend the rice and the cream together with a spatula and fill into a mold or dish as desired. Cover with protective plastic film and refrigerate for at least 3 hours or until needed.

pineapple:

1. Bring all the ingredients except the pineapple to a boil. Add the pineapple and simmer for approximately 5 minutes, remove from the heat and store with the liquid in the refrigerator.
2. Once cold, remove 2 cups of the liquid and reduce by ½, set aside in a cool place until needed.

crisped rice diamonds:

1. Melt the butter over a medium heat. When completely melted, add the marshmallows and sir until completely creamy. Take off the heat and add the rice cereal. Stir until all are coated with the butter/marshmallow mixture.
2. Empty the mixture onto a pastry board. Run your hands under cold water and press the mixture into a rectangle.
3. Cut two pieces of parchment paper to 14" and place the mixture on the center of one piece and cover it with the other. Using a rolling pin, flatten the mixture until it is an ⅛" thick.
4. Once completely cooled, spread a thin layer of the melted chocolate and cool before cutting into 2" diamond shapes.

to serve:

1. Place one slice of pineapple in the center of a diner plate (can be served hot or cold) un-mold the rice pudding and set atop the pineapple then spoon the reduction around.
2. Sprinkle a small amount of granulated sugar on top of the rice pudding and caramelize with a kitchen torch. Garnish with the crisp rice diamonds around the rice pudding.

WARM MANGO TART

BY AARON WRATTEN

These are fairly simple to make. The trick is slicing the mangos very thinly and arranging them nicely on the puff pastry. You don't need all the mango paste for the tarts, but it's very good on bread in the morning too.

WARM MANGO TART

BY AARON WRATTEN

Serves 4

Preparation time: 20 minutes
Cooking time: 15 minutes

ingredients

mango tart:

puff pastry, enough to make four 6" circles

2	large mangos, peeled and cut as close to the pit as possible
4 tbsp	mango paste (see below)
2 tbsp	sugar, for sprinkling

vanilla ice cream (optional)

mango paste: (makes 2 cups)

2 cups	mangos, peeled and roughly chopped
½ tsp	orange, zest
1	orange, juice
½ cup	Turbinado or light brown sugar
1	small cinnamon stick

to serve:

vanilla ice cream (optional)

CHEF'S TIP

If lifting the mango 'circle' fails, simply place the slices one by one in the form of a fan until you get all the way around.

method

mango paste:

Combine the mango, the zest and the orange juice in a blender to make a fine purée. Place in a small pan with the sugar and cinnamon stick. Simmer, stirring frequently, until reduced by about a third, amber in color and jelly-like in consistency. Remove the cinnamon and store covered in the refrigerator for up to a week.

mango tart:

1. Preheat the oven to 450°F. Lay the puff pastry sheets on a lightly floured surface and dust lightly with flour. Roll to ⅛" if necessary. Cut four 6" circles from the pastry using a coffee saucer and a sharp knife. Place the circles on a lightly greased cookie sheet.
2. Cut the mangos to make four fillets. If the fillets are more than 3" wide trim off the excess. Trim off the remaining flesh, if any, from the pit and chop into small pieces. Using a very sharp knife or a good serrated knife, slice the fillets (flat side down) across as thinly as possible. Try to keep them together like a deck of cards.
3. Bring the mango paste to room temperature and stir so that it is the consistency of jelly but not liquid, adding drops of water if necessary. Place a spoonful of mango paste in the middle of each pastry circle. Spread evenly as for a pizza. Place a spoonful of chopped mango in the centers if you have any.
4. Gently fan the mango fillets out: pushing them with cupped hands, form the slices around into a circle, the same size as the pastry. With a wide spatula carefully pick up the circle and place it atop the pastry. Sprinkle lightly with sugar. If possible place the tray on a second empty tray (this will help prevent burning on the bottom). Place in the oven. After 5 minutes, when things begin to bubble, lower the oven to 350°F. Remove as soon as the edges begin to puff and brown, being careful that they do not burn on the bottom.

to serve:

Serve the tart warm with vanilla ice cream.

BLUEBERRY COBBLER

BY CHRISTOPHER BATES

119

My father and I would often go fishing and we spent a lot of time camping. Our meals were pretty simple but one night we would make a dessert. Given the locale, with no oven or mixer, the dessert was alway some form of cobbler baked in a heavy cast iron Dutch oven – the steam keeps everything moist and delicious. Not the most elegant of desserts, but very versatile. Can be made in the oven, on a burner, in a campfire or on the barbecue with whatever seasonal fruit is around. Enjoy.

BLUEBERRY COBBLER

BY CHRISTOPHER BATES

Serves 6

Preparation time: 15 minutes
Cooking time: 30 minutes

ingredients

blueberry filling:

4 cups	wild blueberries (cultivated will work as well, and really any type of fruit can be used)
2 tbsp + 1 tsp	all purpose flour
1 tsp	ground cinnamon
½ cup	sugar
1 tbsp	lemon juice
1 tbsp	melted butter
½ tsp	salt

dough:

2 cup	all purpose flour
¾ tbsp	baking powder
¾ tsp	baking soda
½ cup	sugar
1 tsp	kosher salt
5 tbsp	butter
1 cup	buttermilk

to serve:

Additional sugar and cinnamon for dusting.
wild or fresh herbs

method

blueberry filling:

Toss all the ingredients together to coat in a small bowl. Pour into the bottom of a pie tin, or individual dishes.

dough:

1. Mix together all the dry ingredients in a large bowl. Cube the cold butter and rub into the dry mix by rubbing between thumb and forefinger until the butter is the size of a pea. Add the buttermilk and stir to make a thick batter.
2. Drop heaped spoonfuls of the batter over the blueberries and then dust with cinnamon and sugar if you like. Put in the oven at 350°F for 20-25 minutes until it browns.

to serve:

If individual dishes were used, place directly on a plate and serve, whipped cream or ice cream optional. If prepared in a larger dish, use a large serving spoon to scoop individual portions onto guest's plates. Or, for really informal occasions, it can be set in the center of the table with guests armed with spoon.

camping method:

In a large cast iron dutch oven, fill the bottom with small stones and place the cobbler(s) on the stones, surround with herbs or other aromatics, pour in a ¼ cup of water, cover with the lid and place over medium heat. Once the pot begins to steam, continue cooking. When steam stops coming out, leave on heat for 15 minutes as it begins to bake with dry heat. Continue until well colored.

CARIBBEAN 'CHAUDEAU' & CHURROS

BY STEPHANE MAZIERES

Caribbean specialty that you will also enjoy cooking.

CARIBBEAN 'CHAUDEAU' & CHURROS

BY STEPHANE MAZIERES

Serves 6

Preparation time: 20 minutes
Cooking time: 10 minutes

ingredients

chaudeau:

2 pt	milk
1	vanilla pod
1	cinnamon stick
1	lime, zest
½ oz	ginger, peeled and grated
1 tsp	orange blossom
4	eggs
4½ oz	caster sugar

churros:

9 oz	milk
3½ oz	butter
1	vanilla pod
a pinch	salt
7 oz	wheat flour
3	eggs
sugar, as needed	

CHEF'S TIP
You can use a freezer plastic bag for the churros if you do not have a cuisine piping bag.

method

chaudeau:
1. Put the milk in a saucepan, and add the vanilla pod cut down the middle, the cinnamon stick, zest of lime, the ginger, and orange blossom. Bring to a boil.
2. Mix the eggs and the sugar in a bowl, then pour the milk on top through a large strainer. Whip the mixture, pour into a saucepan and cook at a low temperature until the mixture thickens (test the mixture by placing a finger on the mix on the spatula – it has to show a visible print). Store this cream in the fridge. (During cooking, in case the cream accidentally happens to boil or if small deposits appear, remove the saucepan from the heat, pour the mix in a bowl and mix again with a mixer.)

churros:
1. Put the milk, butter, vanilla pod, and salt together in a saucepan and bring to a boil. Then pour the flour onto the boiling milk and stir constantly with a wooden spatula still on the heat, in order to dry out the dough.
2. 2 minutes later, pour the mixture in a bowl and incorporate the eggs, one by one, until the mix has absorbed them and has become homogeneous. You can either keep it in the fridge for 24 hours or use it immediately.
3. Put the churros mix in a cuisine piping bag and pour into a deep fryer (340°F to 400°F), making sticks of various shapes, and keep them in the deep fryer until they are golden. Remove and drain on absorbent paper.

to serve:
Sprinkle with sugar, icing sugar or cocoa. In a large plate, place a glass of the 'chaudeau' with a straw in it, and do the same in another glass next to the previous one but with the churros in it. Enjoy dipping hot or cold.

DOBERGE CAKE

BY CHAD MARTIN

An elegant dessert brought originally to New Orleans from Europe, the Doberge Cake is available at Hôtel St Germain for any special occasion, either in the hotel or in the guest's home. It is often the choice for luncheons, teas, bridal showers, and even small weddings.

DOBERGE CAKE

BY CHAD MARTIN

Serves 12

Preparation time: 2½ hours
Cooking time: 1 hour

Special equipment: Three 9" round cake pans buttered and floured and lined on the bottom with parchment paper, candy thermometer
Planning ahead: Make the cake one day ahead of time, wrap and cool for easier slicing without tearing.

ingredients

vanilla cake:

2 cups	cake flour
1¾ cup	all purpose flour
2½ tsp	baking powder
1 cup	unsalted butter, semi-softened
3 cups	granulated sugar
¾ tsp	salt
1 tbsp	pure vanilla extract
1 cup	egg whites (reserve the yolks for the buttercream, below)
1½ cups	milk

buttercream:

3 cups	sugar
12	egg yolks
2 lb	unsalted Butter, semi-softened
2 tsp	pure vanilla extract
1 tsp	almond extract
1 tbsp	lemon, zest
1 cup	water

chocolate ganache:

3 cups	bittersweet chocolate, chopped or pistols (coin shapes)
3 cups	heavy cream
1 tbsp	corn syrup

garnish:
raspberries, or edible flowers

method

vanilla cake:

1. Preheat the oven to 350°F. In a large bowl sift the flours together with the baking powder, then set aside. In the bowl of a standing mixer, cream the butter and sugar with the mixing paddle until light and fluffy, then incorporate the salt and vanilla extract. Turn the mixer to low and gradually add the egg whites until incorporated. Alternately add the milk and the flours a little at a time until incorporated and continue to mix for another 30 seconds.

2. Divide the mixture among the three prepared pans and bake in the oven for approximately 45 minutes or until a toothpick inserted comes out clean.

3. Allow the cakes to cool on a wire rack in the pans before inverting them and cooling them overnight in a refrigerator. Once cool, slice each cake horizontally into three layers, totaling nine layers.

buttercream:

1. On a heavy-bottomed saucepan, add the water and the sugar, then cook over a medium-high heat until the temperature reaches 240°F on a candy thermometer.

2. Meanwhile, place the egg yolks in the bowl of a standing mixer and whip on high speed until light and fluffy. Lower the speed of the mixer to medium and slowly drizzle the hot sugar-syrup into the yolks. Continue to whip the egg-sugar mixture on a medium speed until it is cool.

3. Begin whipping the butter into the egg mixture a chunk at a time until it is all incorporated and the buttercream has thickened and has body (sometimes you must refrigerate the entire mixture, in the bowl, and allow to cool more before continuing to mix and emulsifying begins).

4. Incorporate the vanilla and almond extracts and zest.

chocolate ganache:

1. Place the chocolate in a large stainless steel bowl. In a heavy-bottomed saucepan, heat the cream until it begins to simmer around the edges. Pour over the chocolate and allow to sit for a few minutes.

2. Whisk the chocolate and cream together until smooth and then incorporate the corn syrup. Keep in a warm place to prevent solidifying.

to serve:

1. Begin with a layer of cake that came from the bottom of one of the cake pans (this will ensure a flat and level bottom for the cake). Spread an even layer of buttercream over the layer and continue with the remaining layers (it is important to make sure that every layer matches up all the way around the edges for a nice sharp edge).The top layer should again be one of the three bottoms of cake taken from the pans, flat side up.

2. Spread the remainder of the buttercream around the sides of the cake and smooth out as much as possible. Refrigerate the cake on a wire rack until the buttercream hardens, about 30 minutes.

3. Remove the cake from the refrigerator and pour the ganache over the top of the cake. Allow to pour down the sides using a hot spatula to smooth it out. Cool the cake again and repeat with another layer of ganache. Cool, garnish as desired, and bring to room temperature before slicing and serving.

WARM GRANNY SMITH APPLE TART WITH CHEDDAR CHEESE ICE CREAM

BY PATRICK O'CONNELL

This is the most delicate of apple tarts. Apple slices are sautéed briefly in butter, whiskey and cream, then arranged on thin circles of pastry and baked just before serving. A scoop of Cheddar cheese ice cream melting on top makes them even more irresistible. The tarts can be assembled well in advance, refrigerated and baked just before serving.

WARM GRANNY SMITH APPLE TART WITH CHEDDAR CHEESE ICE CREAM

BY PATRICK O'CONNELL

Serves 6

Preparation time: 2 hours
Cooking time: 20 minutes

ingredients

apple tart:
your favorite pie, croissant or puff pastry dough

2	Granny Smith apples, peeled and cored
3 tbsp	unsalted butter
½ tsp	ground cinnamon
2 tbsp	heavy cream
6 tbsp	Southern Comfort
⅓ cup	sugar mixed with 1 rounded tsp cinnamon

Cheddar cheese ice cream:
(yields 1 quart, 6-8 portions)

1 cup	half and half
1 cup	milk
⅔ cup	sugar
freshly ground white pepper, to taste	
½	vanilla bean, split lengthwise
5	egg yolks
2½ cups	shredded mild Cheddar cheese

CHEF'S TIP
A mandoline is an ideal way to slice apples quickly and evenly.

method

apple tart:
1. Preheat the oven to 400°F. On a floured board, roll the dough out to about ⅛" thick. Lay a 5" diameter bowl upside down on the dough and cut out six circles. Place the pastry rounds between sheets of waxed paper and refrigerate.
2. Using a sharp knife, slice the apples into ⅛" sections. In a large sauté pan, melt the butter over a medium heat. Add the apples and cook for several minutes. Add the cinnamon and cream. Carefully add the Southern Comfort, averting your face, as it will ignite. Continue cooking until the apples are soft and pliable. Remove the apples with a slotted spoon and place on a non-reactive baking sheet, then cool. Simmer the cooking liquid until it is reduced by half.
3. Spray several baking sheets with non-stick cooking spray and lay the chilled rounds on them. Place the chilled apple slices in concentric circles around the pastry, leaving a ¼" border at the edges. Roll one apple slice into a tight circle to form a 'rosette' and place in the center of each tart. Dust with the cinnamon sugar and bake for 7 minutes, or until golden brown.

Cheddar cheese ice cream:
1. Combine the half and half, milk, ⅓ cup of sugar, white pepper and vanilla bean. Bring to a boil and remove from the heat. Allow to steep for 5 minutes, then remove the vanilla bean.
2. Whisk the egg yolks and remaining sugar together until thick and foamy. Slowly pour the half and half mixture into the yolk mixture, whisking vigorously until thoroughly incorporated.
3. Set the bowl over a pot of simmering water and cook, whisking constantly, until the mixture coats the back of a spoon. Remove from the heat and whisk in the cheese. Strain to remove any lumps. Cool in the refrigerator, then freeze in an ice cream maker.

to serve:
Serve the tart with a scoop of ice cream on top.

MINIATURE CHOCOLATE BAKED ALASKA

PATRICK O'CONNELL AND MIA PONCE

Our honeybees which live in our "Field of Dreams" next to The Inn inspired this fantasy dessert of a miniature Baked Alaska made to look like a beehive with marzipan bees hovering over it. It's presented under a golden dome of spun sugar and it never fails to delight.

Preparation time:	7 hours, including 4 hours of freezing
Cooking time:	45 minutes

Special equipment:
Ice cream maker, candy thermometer

Planning ahead:
The ice cream can be made up to a week in advance. The cake can be made up to 1 day before freezing. The Alaskas can be shaped and covered in meringue and kept in the freezer for up to 5 days.

ingredients

chocolate ice cream:

6 oz	good quality bittersweet chocolate
1¼ cup	half and half
¾ cup	sugar
1 pinch	salt
6	egg yolks
2¼ cups	heavy cream
½ tsp	vanilla extract

chocolate cake base:

6 oz	good quality bittersweet chocolate
2 tbsp	butter, softened
flour for dusting	
4	eggs, separated
⅓ cup	+ 2 tsp sugar
2 tbsp	all purpose flour
1 pinch	salt

Italian meringue:

1 cup	sugar
⅓ cup	water
5	egg whites, at room temperature

MINIATURE CHOCOLATE BAKED ALASKA

PATRICK O'CONNELL AND MIA PONCE

Serves 6

method

chocolate ice cream:

1. Roughly chop the chocolate with a chef's knife and place it in a stainless steel bowl. Place the bowl over a pot of barely simmering water, making sure that no moisture comes in contact with the chocolate. Stir the chocolate occasionally until it is melted. Mix with a spatula to ensure that all of the chocolate has melted and is very smooth. Set aside in a warm place until ready to use.

2. In a 2 quart heavy bottomed saucepan, combine the half and half, sugar and salt. Bring just to a boil and remove from heat. Place the egg yolks in the top of a double boiler or a large stainless steel bowl and slowly whisk in the hot cream mixture. Set the mixture over a pot of simmering water and whisk until the mixture thickens enough to coat the back of the spoon. Remove from the heat and strain through a fine mesh strainer.

3. Pour the hot half and half mixture in a slow and steady stream into the melted chocolate, whisking constantly until it is fully incorporated. Repeat this process with the heavy cream and vanilla extract.

4. Chill in the refrigerator, then freeze in an ice cream machine according to the manufacturer's instructions.

chocolate cake base:

1. Roughly chop the chocolate with a chef's knife and place it in a stainless steel bowl. Place the bowl over a pot of barely simmering water, making sure that no moisture comes in contact with the chocolate. Stir the chocolate occasionally until it melted. Mix with

a spatula to ensure that all of the chocolate has melted and is very smooth. Set aside in a warm place until ready to use.

2. Pre heat the oven to 350°F and line a cookie sheet completely with aluminum foil. Completely coat the foil with the softened butter and then dust lightly with flour.

3. In the bowl of an electric mixer fitted with a whisk attachment, whip the egg yolks and ½ of the sugar together until pale in color and it forms a thick ribbon. Using a rubber spatula gently fold in the melted chocolate, then the flour and then 1½ teaspoons of hot water.

4. In the clean bowl of an electric mixer fitted with a whisk attachment, whip the egg whites on high speed until they begin to form soft peaks. With the mixer running, add the remaining ½ of the sugar and the salt in a steady stream and continue whipping until the egg whites form medium peaks. Using a rubber spatula gently fold the whites into the chocolate mixture in $^1/_3$s, mixing only until they are just barely combined.

5. Gently spread the batter into the prepared baking sheet. Bake for 5-8 minutes or until the cake is fully baked but not dry. Remove from the oven and cool completely.

Italian meringue:

1. Combine the sugar and water in a small saucepan over medium heat. Cook over medium heat until it registers 245°F on a candy thermometer. Remove from the heat immediately.

2. Meanwhile, place the whites in the bowl of an electric mixer and whip them on a low speed until foamy. Increase the

speed to medium and whisk until soft peaks form.

3. Reduce the speed to low and pour the syrup into the egg whites in a slow and steady stream. Increase the speed to high and whip until the mixture has cooled completely. Use immediately.

to assemble the Alaskas:

1. Using a tea cup or small ramekin as a mold, cut out 6 circles from the cooled cake. Line 6 tea cups with plastic wrap and fill completely with chocolate ice cream. Top with a circle of cake. Press down firmly on the cake to make sure it has contact with the ice cream. Freeze for at least 4 hours.

2. Remove from the cups one at a time from the freezer. Carefully un-mold them using the plastic wrap to help loosen the ice cream. Use the warmth of your hands to gently shape the molded ice cream into a dome.

3. Place the italian meringue in a piping bag fitted with a 6 mm round tip. Pipe concentric circles, starting at the bottom, until the ice cream is completely covered and looks like an old fashioned bee hive. Return each completed dome to the freezer. At this point the completed Alaska's can be held for up to 3 days.

to serve:

Place a beehive in the center of each of 6 chilled serving plates. Using a torch, gently caramelize the meringue until it is toasted but not burned. Allow the ice cream to temper at room temperature for 5 minutes and then serve immediately.

SPUN SUGAR DOME

BY PATRICK O'CONNELL

Preparation time: 1 hour
Cooking time: 15 minutes
Special equipment:
Isomalt sugar, candy thermometer, torch

ingredients

dome & handle:
vegetable spray
3 cups   isolmalt
1 cup   cold water
food coloring paste or powder to the
desired color

method

dome:

1. Begin by lightly coating a dry 4 quart kitchen aid bowl with vegetable spray. Put aside.

2. In a heavy pot combine the isomalt and cold water. Over medium heat cook the syrup until it reaches hard crack stage (310°F-325°F) on a candy thermometer. Add the desired food coloring, preferably a color paste or a powder color and stir until combined. Allow the syrup to cool slightly. Using a fork, quickly drizzle thin strands of the hot syrup across the inside of the bowl and in every direction. The strands should almost completely cover the inside of the bowl. Once finished, allow the sugar to cool completely before releasing, about 5 minutes. Once cooled, gently release the dome, starting at edges of the bowl pulling gently upward until the dome is released. Carefully place it on a dry surface, with the open edges of the dome facing downward.

handle

1. Lightly spray the desired mold with vegetable spray. Melt the remainder of the isomalt, pour into the mold and allow to set, about 10 minutes. Un-mold the shape.

2. To attach the molded handle to the dome, use a torch to heat the edge that will attach to the dome just until it melts, but isn't too hot. Carefully dip that edge of the molded isomalt into the syrup. While hot, place it gently on the top of the dome and hold in place for a few seconds while the sugar sets. Allow to cool completely.

3. The dome should be kept in an airtight container until use.

CHEF'S TIP

Isomalt is a sugar substitute which is primarily used for its sugar-like physical properties, it is the only sugar replacer made from pure sugar beet that tastes as naturally sweet as sugar. Products made with isomalt have the same texture and appearance as those made with sugar. It has been developed for use in sugar sculpture and pulled sugar decorations. When isomalt is used in the recipe, the dome has a shelf life of 1 week, provided it is well wrapped air tight. You can also use granulated sugar in the recipe, following the same directions as below, but its shelf life will be only 1 day.

Note: hard crack sugar is extremely hot and can cause 2nd degree burns. Use caution while working with it and have an ice bath ready in case any of the syrup accidentally pours onto your hands. The ice bath will help prevent any serious injuries.

TRES LECHES CAKE WITH DULCE DE LECHE, KAHLUA & OAXACAN MOCHA CHOCOLATE

BY MICHAEL ROYBAL

This timeless rich dessert has a special creaminess that just melts in the mouth. Sweet and delicious, what more could you want?

TRES LECHES CAKE WITH DULCE DE LECHE, KAHLUA & OAXACAN MOCHA CHOCOLATE

BY MICHAEL ROYBAL

Serves 4

Preparation time:	15 minutes
Cooking time:	1 hour and 2 hours 30 minutes for dulce de leche

Special equipment: 8" x 8" baking pan or can be made in a muffin pan

Planning ahead: The tres leches cake and dulce de leche can be made the day before.

ingredients

cake:
¾ cup	all purpose flour
½ tsp	baking powder
¼ cup	unsalted butter
½ cup	white sugar
3	eggs
¼ tsp	vanilla extract

tres leches:
1 cup	whole milk
7 oz	sweetened condensed milk
6 oz	evaporated milk

whipped cream:
¾ cup	heavy cream
¼ cup	sugar
½ tsp	vanilla extract

dulce de leche:
4 oz	sweetened condensed milk

garnish:
2 tbsp	kahlua
2 tsp	oaxacan chocolate shavings
4	raspberries
mint leaves	

method

cake:
1. Preheat the oven to 350°F. Sift the flour and baking powder together and set aside. Cream the butter and sugar together until fluffy. Add the eggs and the vanilla extract, and beat well. Add the flour mixture to the butter mixture and mix until well blended.
2. To prepare the pan, smear with butter and then coat with flour, discarding any excess. Pour the batter into a prepared pan, cook for 30 minutes, remove from the oven and pierce the cake several times with a fork, then allow to cool.

tres leches:
Combine the whole milk, condensed milk, and evaporated milk, mix well, pour over the cooled cake and allow to soak in.

whipped cream:
In a medium mixing bowl combine the cream, sugar and vanilla extract. Whip on high with a hand mixer until whipped firm.

dulce de leche:
Place the condensed milk in a small double boiler and boil on low, stirring occasionally until it becomes a caramel color, about 2 hours. Allow to cool to room temperature.

to serve:
Portion the cake. 'Scribble' the plates with the dulce de leche. Spoon the kahlua on the center of the plate. Place the cake on the kahlua, and top with cream whipped with the sugar and vanilla extract. Finish with the shaved chocolate and garnish with raspberries and mint leaves.

JEAN-GEORGES'
CHOCOLATE
CAKE

BY JEAN-GEORGES VONGERICHTEN

This recipe was the result of what I thought was a catering disaster. I was serving warm chocolate cake to guests at a party, but when I saw them taking their first bites, I realized that all the cakes had been undercooked. It was the best mistake I ever made. Today, I could never imagine taking this cake off the menu, it's a customer favorite.

JEAN-GEORGES' CHOCOLATE CAKE

BY JEAN-GEORGES VONGERICHTEN

Serves 4

Preparation time: 25 minutes
Cooking time: 7 minutes
Special equipment: Four 4 oz molds, custard cups or ramekins

ingredients

½ cup	butter + some for buttering the molds
4 oz	bittersweet chocolate (preferably Valrhona)
2	eggs
2	egg yolks
¼ cup	sugar
2 tsp	flour + more for dusting

method

1. In the top of a double boiler set over simmering water, heat the butter and chocolate together until the chocolate is almost completely melted. While that's heating, beat together the eggs, yolks, and sugar with a whisk or electric beater until light and thick.

2. Beat together the melted chocolate and butter; it should be quite warm. Pour in the egg mixture, then quickly beat in the flour, just until combined.

3. Butter and lightly flour the molds, custard cups, or ramekins. Tap out the excess flour, then butter and flour them again. Divide the batter among the molds. (At this point, you can refrigerate the desserts until you are ready to eat, for up to several hours; bring them back to room temperature before baking.)

4. Preheat the oven to 450°F. Bake the molds on a tray for 6-7 minutes. The center will still be quite soft, but the sides will be set. Invert each mold on to a plate and let them sit for about 10 seconds. Unmold by lifting up one corner of the mold; the cake will fall out onto the plate.

to serve:

Serve immediately with a smear of chocolate sauce, chocolate crumbs and vanilla-bean ice cream.

FLAMBEED BANANA PANNA COTTA & ITS BRUNOISE, NEW BRUNSWICK MAPLE SUGAR, JULIENNE MINT & ROASTED PECANS

BY GUILLAUME DELAUNE

My kids never turn up their nose at the bananas used to make this dessert. It is their favorite. I encourage you to take the time to properly brunoise the bananas and watch the excitement when it's time to flambé. This original dessert is easier than it sounds.

FLAMBEED BANANA PANNA COTTA & ITS BRUNOISE, NEW BRUNSWICK MAPLE SUGAR, JULIENNE MINT & ROASTED PECANS

BY GUILLAUME DELAUNE

Serves 6

Preparation time: 15 minutes
Planning ahead: You must prepare the
                    panna cotta at least
                    3 hours before serving.

ingredients

caramelized bananas:

2 tbsp	maple sugar
4 tbsp	granulated sugar
2	bananas
1 tbsp	non salted butter
2 tbsp	dark rum

panna cotta:

4 cups	3.25% milk
6 cups	35% cream
1	vanilla bean
5½ oz	sugar
5½	gelatin sheets

brunoise banana garnish:

½	banana (not too ripe)
A squeeze of lemon juice	
8	mint leaves for julienne
¼ cup	roasted pecan nuts

CHEF'S TIP
If this recipe is for very young children you can use less or even no rum - it will be just as good.

method

caramelized bananas:

1. Start a caramel with the two kinds of sugar in a small saucepan on a moderate heat.
2. While waiting for the caramel to cook, cut the bananas in thick ½" slices. When the caramel reaches a light brown colour, add the sliced bananas and slowly roast until a nice darker color. Add the butter and cook for 2 minutes, then flambé with the rum. Reserve in a plate and be sure to keep 6 nice slices of roasted banana for decoration.

panna cotta:

1. Infuse the milk, sugar,cream and vanilla bean with the flambéed banana for 40 minutes. Then blend together and pass through a fine chinois.
2. While it's still hot add the gelatin. Pour into your dishes and let rest for at least 3 hours in the fridge.

banana brunoise garnish:

1. Cut the banana in brunoise (very small dices) and add the lemon. Mix and reserve.
2. Roast the pecans for 5 minutes in an oven at 356°F..

to serve:

Top the panna cotta with the slices of caramelized banana reserved for decoration. Put the brunoise of fresh banana and the mint julienne on top of this and sprinkle with a few roasted pecans. It's ready to enjoy!

MILK CHOCOLATE CREMEUX

PASTRY CHEF RON MENDOZA

Simplicity and elegance. When cooking for friends or family, you should spend more time being a great host and less time in the kitchen. This dish can be made the day before while the finishing garnishes are quick and easy. There is nothing more sensual or gratifying than a smooth and creamy pudding. This dish combines creamy and crunchy textures with sweet and salty flavors, all in one bite.

MILK CHOCOLATE CREMEUX

PASTRY CHEF RON MENDOZA

Serves 8

Preparation time: 30 minutes to prepare. Cool at least 4 hours in fridge.
Planning ahead: Chill over night in the fridge

ingredients

crémeux:

9½ oz	milk chocolate
2 oz	sugar
4	egg yolks
9 oz	milk
9 oz	cream

garnish:
whipped crème fraîche
chocolate cookie crumbles
maple syrup
Maldon sea salt

method

1. Melt the milk chocolate in a microwave safe bowl.
2. In a small bowl, whisk together the sugar and egg yolks. Add the milk and cream and place in a small pot. Warm the custard to a simmer and pour $1/3$ over the chocolate. Mix until thick and shiny. Add another $1/3$ of the custard and mix into chocolate. Finish with remaining custard and mix until the cream is smooth.
3. Strain and pour equal parts into glasses or cups.
4. Chill the chocolate cream at least 8 hours in fridge or preferably overnight.

to serve:
Place a spoonful of whipped crème fraîche in center of chocolate cream. Drizzle with maple syrup, top with cookie crumbles and finish with a pinch of Maldon sea salt.

WALNUT POTICA, PINEAPPLE CHUTNEY & CREAM CHEESE FROSTING

BY NATHAN RICH AND MATTHEW ZAREMBSKI

This dish finds inspiration from a treasured Zarembski family recipe passed through many generations. It is a take on an annually enjoyed treat with strong Croatian roots.

WALNUT POTICA, PINEAPPLE CHUTNEY & CREAM CHEESE FROSTING

BY NATHAN RICH AND MATTHEW ZAREMBSKI

Serves 4

Preparation time: 6 hours
Cooking time: 2 hours
Special equipment: Kitchen Aid

ingredients

potica dough:

1¼ tbsp	fresh yeast
¼ cup	warm whole milk
1 tbsp	white sugar
5 cups	all purpose flour
3	eggs
½ cup	butter
¾ cup	white sugar
¾ tbsp	salt

potica filling:

7 cups	fine ground walnuts
2 cups	white sugar
½ cup	pineapple preserve
½ tsp	salt
1 tsp	ground cinnamon
1 tbsp	vanilla paste
½ cup	pineapple preserve
3	eggs
¾ cup	whole milk

pineapple preserve and chutney:

1	pineapple
½ cup	white sugar
½ cup	Malibu rum
¼ cup	white wine vinegar
½	vanilla pod

candied walnuts:

As needed whole walnuts
Ample as needed white sugar
As needed water

cream cheese frosting:

1¼ lb	cream cheese
2¼ cup	powdered sugar
⅓ cup	cream
¼ cup	orange juice
1 tsp	powdered cinnamon
1 tsp	vanilla paste

method

potica dough:

1. Dissolve the yeast into a mixture of the warm milk and tablespoon of sugar. Cover the mixture and allow the yeast to activate. (About 15 minutes),
2. Except for the salt, place the activated yeast mixture and the remaining ingredients into the mixer. Once a loose dough has formed the salt may be added. Work the dough until a strong gluten net has formed. Roll the dough into a tightly formed ball, wrap it, and proof it.

potica filling:

Mix together the dry ingredients. Mix together the wet ingredients. Combine the two mixtures.

potica loaf:

1. Lightly dust the surface to be worked on with flour. (Repeat if necessary).
2. Roll each proofed portion of dough no wider than the length of the pan it is to be baked in. Roll the length of the portion as thin as possible. The thinner the dough, the better the final product will be.
3. Lightly and evenly spread the filling over the entire surface each portion of dough. (To the edges).
4. Beginning at either narrow end of the portion, begin to roll the loaf. Be sure to roll over the filling and tuck the dough back. Maintain a consistent and tight roll.
5. Place the rolled loaf inside of its baking pan and cover it. Proof the dough a second time (about 20 minutes).
6. Bake the potica first uncovered at 325°F for 15 minutes on low fan.
7. Turn the oven down to 300°F and cover each loaf with aluminum foil. Bake for an additional 20-25 minutes on low fan.

pineapple preserve and chutney:

1. Place the sugar, rum, vinegar and vanilla in a pan. Heat to dissolve the sugar and make a syrup. Reduce the syrup to thick. Add the pineapple scraps and candy until transparent.
2. Once cool, rough chop the mix.

candied walnuts:

1. Moisten the first allotment of sugar, keeping in mind that an ample amount of syrup must be had in ratio to the amount of nuts being poached. Adding too many nuts to the syrup allotted will cause the syrup to seize.
2. Place the sugars into a large pot and place them over high heat to dissolve them into a syrup. Cook the syrup to a dark caramel.
3. Add the nuts to the syrup.
4. Maintain the temperature of the heat source and lightly stir the mixture as the syrup returns to its fluid temperature.
5. When the nuts become aromatic, pour the mixture out over a draining rack collecting the hot syrup below.
6. Once all the excess syrup has been separated from the nuts; in small increments, toss the nuts (while still hot) in an ample amount of sugar.

cream cheese frosting:

1. Paddle the cream cheese until smooth. Add the remaining ingredients and paddle to smooth. Switch to the whip attachment and whip the frosting to stiff peaks.
2. Allow the mix to rest & firm in the fridge before use.

to serve:

Slice the potica thin and lightly brush each slice with butter. Toast the slices in the oven at 325°F for 5-7 minutes.

159

WILD RICE BRULEE WITH PARTRIDGE BERRIES, GINGER CRUMBLE & BUTTERMILK SORBET

BY SARAH VILLAMERE

Rice pudding is eaten all over the world; particularly in countries where rice is a staple element to a meal. In my travels, I have tasted a variety of puddings, all with varying garnishes, but with a few common components- it's comforting, warming and familiar.

In trying to create a dessert that would satisfy the same way, I wanted to stay true to the ingredients that are available to us here in Canada, thus providing us with a rice pudding that is well balanced and unlike any we've ever tasted.

Preparation time: 1½ hours
Cooking time: 20 minutes
Special equipment: Ice cream machine or Pacojet, blow torch

Planning ahead: If you cannot find partridge berries, cranberries are a fine substitute. Store bought ginger snap cookies are fine to crumble up at home if you're not inclined to make gingerbread dough and bake it. Store bought frozen yogurt can be used in the place of buttermilk sorbet. Cook the wild rice in advance.

ingredients

cooked wild rice:

4½ oz	wild rice
½ cup	water
½ cup	apple cider

wild rice brûlée:

3 oz	short grain rice
3 cups	homogenized milk
pinch	salt
1	egg
2 oz	brown sugar
1 tbsp	vanilla extract
zest of 1	lemon
1 tsp	cinnamon
4 oz	cooked wild rice

partridge berry compote:

4 oz	partridge berries, fresh or frozen
4 oz	white sugar
½	cinnamon stick
½	vanilla bean
1 strip	orange zest

baume syrup:

1 quart	water
1 lb 5 oz	sugar
8 oz	liquid glucose

buttermilk sorbet:

2 cups	buttermilk
2 cups	baume syrup

puffed wild rice:

½ cup	canola oil
1 oz	wild rice

gingersnap crumble:

1 lb 2 oz	all purpose flour
10 oz	brown sugar
1 oz	baking soda
1 oz	cinnamon
1 oz	ground ginger
7g	ground cloves
1 pinch	salt
12 oz	unsalted butter
4½ oz	molasses
1	egg

to serve:

2 tbsp	gingersnap crumble
1 tbsp	puffed wild rice
1 tsp	partridge berry compote
1½ tbsp	turbinado sugar for torching the top of the pudding
baby chervil for garnish	

WILD RICE BRULEE WITH PARTRIDGE BERRIES, GINGER CRUMBLE & BUTTERMILK SORBET

BY SARAH VILLAMERE

Serves 2

method

cooked wild rice:

1. In a small pot, bring the rice, water and apple cider to a boil and reduce the heat to low. Simmer for 20 minutes, or until the rice is very cooked.
2. Remove from the heat and allow to cool until needed.

rice pudding:

1. In a medium heavy-bottom pot, cook the rice, milk and salt on a medium heat for 20 minutes or until the rice is tender. Stir occasionally to ensure the rice does not burn.
2. While the rice is cooking, combine the egg, brown sugar and vanilla in a bowl. Once the rice is cooked, temper a small amount of the rice into the egg mixture whilst whisking and add back into the pot. Place the rice pudding back onto a medium heat and cook for a further 2 minutes.
3. Finally, add the lemon zest, cinnamon and fold in the cooked wild rice.

partridge berry compote:

1. If using frozen berries, make sure they are completely thawed before cooking. Place all the ingredients in a medium pot over a medium-low heat. Cook for about 10 minutes until the sugar is dissolved, but do not cook the berries down too far.
2. Remove from the heat and allow the flavors of the spices to infuse while the compote cools.

baume syrup:

Bring the water, sugar and liquid glucose to a boil until the sugar has dissolved. Allow to cool until needed.

buttermilk sorbet:

1. Combine the buttermilk and syrup. Be sure to check the manufacturer's instructions before using an ice cream machine and proceed accordingly.
2. If using a Pacojet, divide the sorbet base between 2 canisters and freeze for at least 8 hours or over night. Once it has been completely frozen, process in the Pacojet before use.

puffed wild rice:

Heat the oil in a small fry pan and toss in the rice. Keep the pan moving constantly while the rice begins to crackle and puff. Remove immediately onto a paper towel to drain the excess oil. This will happen very quickly, about 15 seconds is all it takes to cook the rice, so it can burn before you know it.

gingersnap crumble:

1. Sift all the dry ingredients together and set aside. Cream the butter and sugar and as soon as they are combined, add the egg and blend. Slowly add the dry ingredients in 3 additions and mix until the dough is formed. Wrap the dough in plastic wrap and allow to chill for 10 minutes.
2. Next, divide the dough into manageable portions and roll it out to about ¼" thickness. Place on a baking tray lined with silpat or parchment paper and bake for 10 minutes at 325°F.
3. Once baked, allow to cool before breaking it up into smaller portions. Crumble the cookie in a food processor by pulsing it or you can bash it up with a rolling pin.
4. Re-bake the crumble for a further 7 minutes at the same temperature.

Remove from the oven and allow to cool again. Put the crumbs back into the food processor and pulse until a finer crumb is achieved- almost like a coarse cornmeal. Store in an air tight container for 2 weeks.

to serve:

1. Rice pudding can be served warm, cold or at room temperature. I like to serve this one warm.
2. In a medium sauce pan, gently heat the pudding whilst stirring. Once it is warmed through, spoon onto a serving plate and sprinkle a layer of turbinado sugar on the surface. Torch until the sugar is evenly caramelized.
3. Top the pudding with the ginger crumble and a few small dollops of the partridge berry compote.
4. Serve a quenelle of buttermilk sorbet on top of the crumble and finish with the puffed wild rice and a few sprigs of baby chervil.

FRESH COCONUT FLAN

BY MAURICIO ESPINOSA

A deliciously creamy tropical dessert beautifully paired with exotic fruits.

FRESH COCONUT FLAN

BY MAURICIO ESPINOSA

Serves 4

Preparation time: 10 minutes
Cooking time: 1 ½ hours

ingredients

2 cups	whipping cream
1 oz	eggs
1 oz	egg yolks
¾ cups	coconut cream
2 oz	chopped coconut
4 oz	Philadelphia cheese

garnish:
kiwi slices
plums
litchis
strawberries
raspberries
blackberries
coconut slices
mint leaf or peppermint

method

1. Preheat the oven to 300°F.
2. Boil the whipping cream and eggs. Put the additional egg yolks in a separate bowl and stir in 2 tablespoons of the boiled whipping cream. Gradually incorporate the rest of the whipping cream.
3. Liquidize the coconut cream, chopped coconut and the Philadelphia cheese and add to the cream and egg mix. Pour into an ovenproof dish and cook in the oven for approximately 1½ hours.

to serve:
Spoon into glasses and decorate with mixed fruit of your choice.

MAPLE PARFAIT, BLACKBERRIES & BANANA FRITTERS

BY ANGELE RACICOT

Nothing says Québec like maple syrup. Here, we incorporate the golden nectar into a velvety decadent dessert.

MAPLE PARFAIT, BLACKBERRIES & BANANA FRITTERS

BY ANGELE RACICOT

Serves 6

Preparation time: 1 hour
Cooking time: 30 minutes

ingredients

maple parfait:
¾ cup	medium maple syrup
3	eggs
1 ⅛ cup	35%, cream softly whipped

blackberry purée:
¾ lb	frozen blackberries
1 oz	sugar
1 pinch	salt

to serve:
fresh blackberries
dried banana chips

CHEF'S TIP
To make unmolding the parfait easier, cover the bottom and sides of your freezer container with cling film, making sure to eliminate air bubbles. To make a nice round ball shape with the banana fritters, roll each piece into the palm of your hand to make a regular small ball after dredging in the Japanese Panko flour and before frying.

method

maple parfait:
1. Beat the eggs with a hand mixer. Heat the maple syrup lightly. Transfer the eggs into a stainless steel bowl and cook them on a medium heat while adding the maple syrup in a fine stream. Stir constantly until the mixture forms a thick ribbon when dropped from a spoon onto the remaining batter.
2. Pour the mixture into a standing mixer and whip it on speed 2 until it has cooled down. Then add the cream.
3. Pour the mixture into the large containers and leave in the freezer for 24 hours.

blackberry purée:
1. Heat the blackberries slowly to soften. Mix briefly with a hand mixer, stopping before the blackberry seeds become puréed. Pass the mixture through a fine sieve.
2. Then finish cooking the purée while adding sugar and a pinch of salt. Reduce on a medium heat for 10 minutes.

to serve:
Unmold the maple parfait and cut it in squares. Using a spoon or a squeeze bottle, dot some blackberry purée onto one side of your dessert plate. Place the maple parfait in the center of the plate. Garnish with dry banana and fresh blackberries.

AFFOGATO

BY MICHAEL WHITE

Affogato to me is the quintessential Italian dessert. Like Italian cuisine in general, its simplicity allows its ingredients to shine. Be sure to use very strong espresso, quality Amaro and preferably homemade or delicious store-bought gelato. The acidity of the espresso is curtailed by the creaminess of the rich gelato. Try and dig to the bottom of the glass and taste all three components in one bite!

AFFOGATO

BY MICHAEL WHITE

Serves 1

Cooking time: 20 minutes

ingredients

vanilla bean gelato:
(makes 1 quart)

3 cups	whole milk
1 cup	heavy cream
1 cup	granulated sugar
3	vanilla beans, split lengthwise seeds scraped, or 3 tbsp vanilla extract
3	large egg yolks

to serve:

½ oz	Ramazotti Amaro
1	large scoop vanilla gelato, see recipe above
1 shot	freshly brewed espresso

method

vanilla bean gelato:

1. Combine the milk, cream and sugar in a medium-sized nonreactive saucepan. Add the vanilla beans and seeds to mixture, or add the vanilla bean extract. Bring the mixture to a boil over medium heat, stirring from time to time, until the sugar is dissolved, about 10 minutes.
2. Meanwhile, beat the egg yolks in a small bowl. Slowly whisk ½ cup of the hot milk-cream mixture into the yolks, then return the warmed yolks to the milk-cream mixture, stirring continuously. Reduce the heat to medium-low and cook, stirring constantly for about 20 minutes until the mixture is thick enough to coat the back of a wooden spoon or measures 190°F on an instant-read thermometer.
3. Remove the pan from the heat and pour the mixture through a fine strainer into a metal bowl. Put the bowl on another bowl partially filled with ice and stir to chill completely. Transfer the liquid to the canister of an ice cream maker and freeze according to the manufacturer's instructions for gelato.
4. When frozen, transfer the gelato to an airtight container and store in the freezer.

to serve:
Pour the ramazotti amaro into a tall coffee cup, preferably crystal so that it allows you to see inside the dessert. Place the scoop of gelato in the bottom of the glass. Finish with a shot of freshly brewed espresso.

CREAMY VANILLA BREAD PUDDING

BY BARBARA LYNCH

When I make this rich and comforting dessert at my restaurant, I keep a second pan in reserve for snacking since my chefs are always stealing little spoonfuls. Its ridiculous how good the bread pudding is with two sauces and Chantilly cream. This pudding is more about the creamy custard than it is about the bread. I like the double whammy of using both the vanilla bean and the vanilla extract.

CREAMY VANILLA BREAD PUDDING

BY BARBARA LYNCH

Serves 8

Preparation time: 50 minutes
Cooking time: 1 hour

ingredients

bread pudding:

3 cups	heavy cream
1	vanilla bean
¼ tsp	kosher salt
5 slices	white bread, cubed
4	large eggs
¾ cup	sugar
1 tsp	pure vanilla extract

chantilly cream:

1 cup	heavy cream
1 tbsp	confectioner's sugar
½ tsp	pure vanilla extract
kosher salt	

creamy caramel sauce:

1 cup	sugar
1 cup	heavy cream

fresh fig sauce:

1 cup	brandy
1 cup	sugar
1	cinnamon stick
1 pt	ripe fresh figs, halved or quartered if large

method

bread pudding:

1. In a medium saucepan, heat the cream over a low heat. Split the vanilla bean lengthwise with the tip of a paring knife and scrape the seeds out into the cream. Add the bean to the pot too. Stir in the salt and heat the cream until warm to the touch. Take the pot off the heat and let the vanilla bean steep for ½-1 hour.

2. Pile the bread cubes into a 9"x13" baking dish, distributing them more or less evenly.

3. In the bowl of a stand mixer fitted with the whisk attachment or using a hand mixer, whisk together the eggs and sugar on a medium speed until the mixture is light yellow in color and falls from the beater in thick ribbons, about 15 minutes. Add the vanilla extract.

4. Remove the vanilla bean pod from the cream mixture, whisking constantly. Then pour the egg-cream mixture into the saucepan with the remaining cream and whisk it together. Strain the cream mixture through a fine mesh strainer over the bread cubes in the baking dish. Give the pan a gentle shake to be sure all is distributed well and then let the bread absorb the custard for at least 30 minutes before baking. If baking the bread pudding right away, heat the oven to 350°F with a rack in the center. If not, cover it with plastic wrap and refrigerate it.

5. When ready to bake, set the bread pudding dish in a larger roasting pan. Add hot water to the roasting pan until the water is halfway up the sides of the baking dish. Bake in the center of the oven until the custard is just firm, 50 minutes-1 hour (begin checking earlier; give the pan a gentle shake and take it out of the oven when the custard is no longer jiggly). Let it cool a bit.

Chantilly cream:

In the bowl of a stand mixer fitted with the whisk attachment or using a hand mixer, combine the cream, sugar, vanilla extract and a pinch of salt. Whisk the ingredients together, gently at first and then increasing the speed until you can lift out the stopped whisk and leave behind peaks just shy of firm. Be careful not to over beat, however, or you will get a very sweet butter.

creamy caramel sauce:

1. Combine the sugar with a ¼ cup of water in a medium saucepan. Dissolve the sugar over a medium heat, stirring until the mixture is clear. Increase the heat to high and cook, swirling the pan to cook evenly but no longer stirring until the caramel is a deep amber. (Check the color by carefully drizzling some onto a white plate.) Don't worry if the sugar hardens while cooking; simply stir it and continue cooking until it smooths out.

2. Take the pot off the heat and carefully whisk in the cream. The caramel will sputter, so be careful as it is very hot. Return the sauce to the heat and bring to a boil, whisking constantly until smooth, 2-3 minutes. Cool a little before serving but serve warm.

fresh fig sauce:

In a medium saucepan, combine the brandy, sugar, 1 cup of water and the cinnamon stick. Bring to a boil over a medium to high heat and cook until reduced by half. addd the figs and cook, stirring occasionally until the figs soften and absorb the flavor of the liquid, about 10 minutes. Serve warm.

to serve:

Put a serving of the pudding in a large dish and top with fig sauce, caramel sauce and a dollop of Chantilly cream.

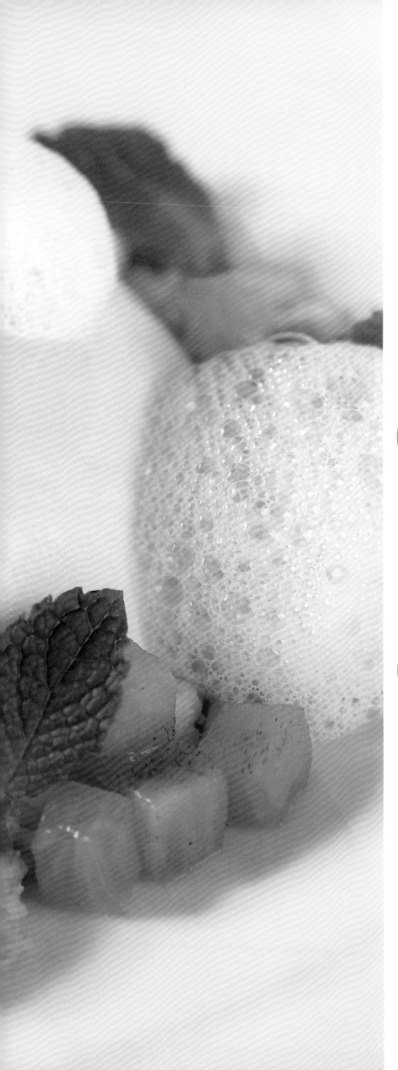

ORANGE BLOSSOM HONEY PANNA COTTA

BY MAYRA VICTORIA

Summer in a dish, this orange blossom honey panna cotta is a sure winner with all. The smooth silky panna cotta and the hazy orange blossom honey are the ultimate combination for any dessert.

ORANGE BLOSSOM HONEY PANNA COTTA

BY MAYRA VICTORIA

Serves 4

Preparation time: 4 hours 30 minutes
Cooking time: 40 minutes

Special equipment: 4 silicone molds with 4 ounce cavities (if possible the half dome but any other shape will work – if you don't have silicone molds ramekins will do), a mixer with a paddle attachment.

ingredients

panna cotta:

2½ oz	orange blossom honey or clove honey
1²/₃ cups	heavy cream
½ cup	milk
3	gelatin leaves

pine nut streusel:

2 oz	butter (ice cold and cut into ½" cubes)
2 oz	all purpose flour
2 oz	ground pine nuts (grind in a spice grinder with 2 tbsp of all purpose flour)
2 oz	confectioner's sugar
⅛ tsp	salt

mint poached persimmons:

3	medium-sized Fuyu persimmons, peeled and small diced
4 oz	water
4 oz	sugar
2	mint sprig
¼ tsp	lime juice

garnish:
toasted pine nuts

method

panna cotta:

1. In a medium-sized pot combine the milk, cream and honey and bring to a boil over a medium heat. Meanwhile, in a small bowl filled with water and a couple of ice cubes, place your gelatin leaves to 'bloom'.
2. Once the cream mixture boils take the gelatin leaves, squeeze out any excess water, add to the pot, and whisk until dissolved. Quickly pour the mixture into a medium bowl sitting inside a larger bowl filled with water and ice (an ice bath). Constantly stir while the mixture cools down until it resembles a loose yogurt consistency.
3. Carefully pour the mixture into the molds and place in a freezer for a minimum of 4 hours. Once frozen take out of the molds and place onto a parchment lined baking tray. Allow to thaw in the refrigerator.

pine nut streusel:

1. Preheat the oven to 325°F, place a rack on the middle shelf. In the bowl of a mixer fitted with the paddle attachment, place the dry ingredients. On a low to medium speed paddle the dry ingredients to evenly distribute them. Add all the cold butter at once and watch closely as you mix for 5-7 minutes. The mixture should resemble small pebbles.
2. Remove from the mixer and spread over a parchment lined baking pan. Bake in the oven for about 8 minutes.

3. Remove from the oven and, with a whisk, toss the crumble to distribute and break apart.
4. Return to the oven and continue to bake for 5 more minutes. Repeat the process with the whisk and finish baking for 3 minutes or until golden brown.

mint poached persimmons:

1. In a small pot bring the water and sugar to a boil. Off the heat add the mint sprigs and allow to infuse for 5 minutes. Strain out the mint and add the lime juice.
2. Bring back to a low simmer and add the persimmons. Poach the persimmons for about 8 minutes. Pour the persimmons and syrup into a small bowl sitting in a larger bowl with water and ice in it to cool down immediately.

to serve:

1. Take four soup bowls and with a wide spatula gently lift one panna cotta from the baking tray and place in the center of the bowl. Repeat with the others.
2. Using a spoon take some of the persimmons with none of the syrup and place around the base of the panna cotta in small clusters.
3. Sprinkle some of the pine nut streusel and toasted pine nuts over the panna cotta and around the base. Serve and enjoy.

PORT CHERRIES

BY CHRISTOPHER KOSTOW

 These cherries make a great, easy accompaniment to any full flavored cheese – they work equally well with a blue cheese as with a Cheddar.

PORT CHERRIES

BY CHRISTOPHER KOSTOW

Serves 8

ingredients

subhead:

1	bottle of ruby port (75 cl)
2	cinnamon sticks
3	star anise
10 oz	dried cherries

method

Place the port, cinnamon, and star anise in a pot and reduce the liquid by half. Pour hot over the dried cherries and let the liquid cool to room temperature before refrigerating. Store the cherries in the liquid.

to serve:
Serve with your favorite cheese.

POACHED PEAR & HAZELNUT FRANGIPANE TARTLET

BY KOSTA STAICOFF

 This is a combination of some of the most memorable ingredients that I grew up with in the Rogue Valley of southern Oregon. Served warm or cold, for an indulgent breakfast or rustic dessert, this one reminds me of being a kid.

POACHED PEAR & HAZELNUT FRANGIPANE TARTLET

BY KOSTA STAICOFF

Serves 6

Preparation time: 1 hour
Cooking time: 20 minutes

ingredients

poached pears:

3	ripe bartlett pears
4 cups	water
1 cup	white wine
8 oz	sugar
1	cinnamon stick
½	lemon, juice and zest
½	orange, juice and zest

sugar paste:

1 cup	all purpose flour
1 cup	butter
¾ cup	icing sugar
sea salt, to taste	
4	egg yolks

hazelnut frangipane:

½ cup	butter
½ cup	sugar
1 tbsp	flour
½ cup	roasted, finely ground hazelnuts
1 tsp	vanilla extract
2	egg yolks

tuile spiral:

2 oz	butter, softened
2 oz	icing sugar
3 oz	all purpose flour
3	egg whites

vanilla froth:

1 cup	fat free milk
1½ oz	sugar
½	vanilla pod, scraped

CHEF'S TIP
To prepare larger quantities of the pears submerge each after peeling in water and lemon juice before poaching.

method

poached pears:
1. Bring all the ingredients except the pears to a boil for a syrup and reduce the heat to a simmer. Peel the pears and add quickly and carefully.
2. Ensure they are covered and poach for 20 minutes, turning them every few minutes. Remove and allow to cool in the syrup.

sugar paste:
Sift the flour and combine with the butter, add the sugar and salt. Add the egg yolks and combine. Work the dough in by hand until smooth then wrap and refrigerate for 1 hour.

hazelnut frangipane:
1. Beat the butter and the sugar together until light in texture. Combine the flour, hazelnuts and vanilla and add one-third to the butter/sugar, then add one egg yolk and another third of the dry ingredients.
2. When combined, add the second egg yolk and the last of the dry ingredients and mix until fully combined.

tuile spiral:
1. Preheat the oven to 350°F. Mix the butter, sugar and flour together then slowly add the egg whites until incorporated. Place 1 teaspoon of the mix onto a silpat or parchment paper and with the back of the spoon smooth out evenly to a ½" x 5" rectangle.
2. Bake until light brown, remove from the oven and quickly wrap each one pan side first around the rounded handle of a wooden spoon to form the spiral shape.

vanilla froth:
Using a hand-held mixer, blend all the ingredients to a froth.

to serve:
1. Lightly butter 3¾" tartlet tins. Roll out the sugar paste to ⅛" thick. Using a round pastry cutter, cut circles slightly bigger than the tins and line them.
2. Place onto a baking tray and fill one-third with frangipane. Halve each pear, remove the stem and seeds, cut into a fan and trim to fit each tartlet.
3. Bake for 20 minutes or until browned. Serve with a tuile spiral and vanilla froth.

OCEAN HOUSE CREME BRULEE

BY ADAM YOUNG

At the hotel we try to implement a balance between classical and contemporary dessert presentation for our variety of venues. The crème brûlée seemed an obvious choice for our clubroom on property. This custard can be flavored with herbs, fruit purées and a variety of liqueurs, resulting in an ever changing seasonally inspired classic dish.

OCEAN HOUSE CREME BRULEE

BY ADAM YOUNG

Serves 6

Preparation time: 20 minutes
Cooking time: 25 minutes
Special equipment: Blow torch

ingredients

6 cups	heavy cream
1½ each	vanilla bean
6 oz	sugar
13 oz	egg yolks

method

1. Combine the heavy cream and vanilla beans and heat until simmering.
2. In a large bowl, mix the sugar and the egg yolks. Slowly add the hot cream into the yolks while whisking. Pour the custard into shallow ramekins and place the ramekins into a baking pan. Pour water into the pan so that it comes to about half way up the side of the ramekins.
3. Cover with aluminum foil and bake at 300ºF until the custard no longer jiggles in the middle.
4. Cool, then pour an even layer of sugar over the top and torch until the sugar is melted and golden brown.
5. Serve as shown.

ROASTED PINEAPPLE, EXOTIC FRUIT, ALMOND CAKE, COCONUT MALIBU ICE CREAM

BY JOACHIM SPLICHAL & TONY ESNAULT

197

Inspired by America's favorite dessert of cake and ice cream, Chefs Joachim and Tony incorporate tropical flavors to provide a light and tasty ending to a Patina meal.

ROASTED PINEAPPLE, EXOTIC FRUIT, ALMOND CAKE, COCONUT MALIBU ICE CREAM

BY JOACHIM SPLICHAL & TONY ESNAULT

Serves 4

Preparation time: 15 minutes
Cooking time: 3 hours

Special equipment: Pacojet, dehydrator, microplane, rectangle mold 10" x 5"
Planning ahead: The roasted pineapple, ice cream, almond cake batter, and dry pineapple chips can all be made in advance.

ingredients

roasted pineapple:

1	pineapple, peeled and cut in eights length wise
1	vanilla bean
2 cups	sugar
¼ cup	water

almond cake:

1 cup	almond paste
1/3 cup	melted butter
2	whole eggs
1/8 tsp	vanilla extract

coconut Malibu ice cream:

2 cans	coconut milk
8 oz	sugar
1 tsp	lime juice
1 tsp	Malibu rum

tapioca sauce:

¼ cup	coconut milk
1/3 cup	milk
1 tsp	sugar
2 tsp	tapioca
1 tsp	butter

pineapple chips:

1 cup	sugar
1 cup	water
4	thin slices of pineapple

garnish:

1	mango
1	Hawaiian papaya
1	kiwi
3	coquitos
1 tbsp	napage (clear glaze)
1	passion fruit
1	lime zest

method

roasted pineapple:

1. Preheat the oven to 350°F. In a medium cocotte make a dry caramel with the sugar, add the vanilla bean, and deglaze with the water. Add the pineapple, cover and put in the oven for 3 hours or until it is a caramel color.
2. Once cooked let it cool down, then chop finely to make a compote.

almond cake:

1. Preheat the oven to 350°F fan. In a mixer mix the almond paste with the paddle until soft, add the melted butter, add the eggs one at a time then add the vanilla extract.
2. Let it sit in a refrigerator then, using a pastry bag and a rectangle mold, pipe the mix in a flat shape on a baking sheet and then bake for 10 minutes.

coconut Malibu ice cream:

1. In a saucepot heat the coconut milk and the sugar until the sugar melts. Cool it down then mix with the rest of the ingredients put the mixture in Pacojet containers and freeze.
2. Overnight, right before you need it spin in the Pacojet.

tapioca sauce:

In a saucepot bring to a boil the milk, coconut milk, and sugar, add the tapioca and move to a lower temperature, mixing constantly until the tapioca is cooked, then add the butter. Cool down and fix the consistency if necessary with milk.

pineapple chips:

In a saucepot put the sugar and the water, bring to a boil and set aside. Put the slices of pineapple in the sugar and water mixture, arrange them in the tray of the dehydrator and let them dry for at least 24 hours until crisp.

garnish:

Cut the mango in thin slices, the papaya in small batons, kiwi in small dice and, using a mandoline, slice the coquitos and toast them in the oven for 1 minute. Mix some napage with the lime zest.

to serve:

1. Spread the pineapple compote over the cake and cut in rectangles 1½" x 5".
2. Serve on a room temperature plate topped with the fruits to garnish.
3. Add sauce and ice cream topped with a pineapple chip.

> **CHEF'S TIP**
> If you don't have a dehydrator you can use the oven at a low temperature instead.

STICKY TOFFEE PUDDING WITH CUSTARD ICE CREAM

ELWYN BOYLES

 We wanted to show the beauty of an English favorite! But we wanted to put a little twist on it, turning the normal hot custard into an ice cream.

STICKY TOFFEE PUDDING WITH CUSTARD ICE CREAM

ELWYN BOYLES

Serves 10

Preparation time: 1½ hours
Cooking time: 30 minutes

ingredients

pudding:

4 cups	water
11 lbs	pitted Medjool dates
1½ lbs	butter
5 lbs	brown sugar
5½ cups	eggs, pooled whole eggs
1½ cups	reserved date base
5½ cups	all purpose flour
5½ cups	bread flour
3 tbsp	baking powder
1 tbsp	baking soda

custard ice cream:

2 ³/₅ quarts	whole milk
1¼ cups	granulated sugar
½ cup	trimoline
½ cup	glucose
1	vanilla bean
zest 1	lemon
5 oz	custard powder
1 cup	milk
2 cups	granulated sugar
24 ea	egg yolks
4 cups	cream

toffee sauce:

4 cups	granulated sugar
1 cup	water
2 cups	heavy cream
2	vanilla pods
zest 1	lemon

method

pudding:

1. Bring the water to a boil and add the pitted Medjool dates. Allow to steep for 30 minutes and purée in a blender. Reserve 6lb of this "date base."
2. In a standing mixer, cream the butter and brown sugar and then add the eggs one at a time. Emulsify into the date base this butter, sugar and egg mixture. Add the sifted, dry ingredients and bake at 375°F for approximately 30 minutes.

ice cream:

1. Bring the milk, sugar, trimoline, glucose, vanilla bean and lemon zest to the boil. Make a slurry with the custard powder, milk and 1 cup of sugar. Add to the liquid whilst whisking and bring back to the boil.
2. In a separate bowl whisk together the egg yolks and 1 cup of sugar and temper with the hot cream mixture. Cook like an Anglaise until it has a custard consistency. Add the cream and chill thoroughly- for approximately 1 hour before spinning in an ice cream machine to manufacturer's instructions.

toffee sauce:

Place the sugar in a sauce pan and heat to a caramel. Then add the water to arrest the cooking, followed by the cream and the vanilla pods. Bring to a full boil and add the lemon zest. Immediately pass through a chinois and keep warm to serve.

to serve:

Let the pudding cool to room temperature and then slice to the desired size. In a small pot heat the toffee sauce and place in a saucier to be served at the table. Quenelle the ice cream and place on top of the pudding.

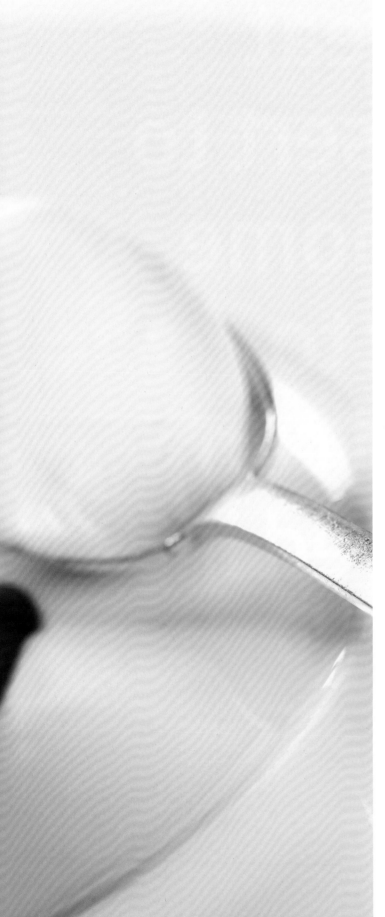

ZEPPOLES

BY ELWYN BOYLES AND
ALESSANDRA ALTIERI

A great dessert to make at home, very easy to make and can be prepared in advance.

ZEPPOLES

BY ELWYN BOYLES AND ALESSANDRA ALTIERI

makes approximately 50 zeppoles

Preparation time: 15 minutes
Cooking time: 5 minutes per zeppoles

ingredients

zeppoles:

2 cups	water
1 tsp	salt
4 tbsp	light brown sugar
$\frac{1}{3}$ lb	butter
2 cups	all purpose flour
7	eggs
oil, for frying	
granulated sugar, for dusting	

CHEF'S TIP
After cooking, move the zeppoles onto a sheet pan lined with paper towels to soak up any additional excess oil.

method

zeppoles:

1. In a medium saucepan, bring the water, salt, sugar, and butter to a boil. Pour in the flour. With a wooden spoon, quickly stir until the mixture starts to come together. Once that begins, turn the heat off and continue to cook in the hot pan until the lumps of flour disappear and the dough begins to form a smooth ball. Pour into a standing mixer fitted with the paddle attachment on very low speed, for about 1 minute, to cool slightly.

2. Slowly start adding the eggs in two at a time, but do not add the next eggs until the previous ones are fully incorporated. Scrape down the bowl occasionally. Continue to mix on very low speed until everything is fully combined. Remove the mixture from the bowl and place into a pastry bag fitted with a #14 star tip.

3. Fill a medium-sized pot one-third of the way full with oil. Put over a medium heat and hold the oil between 355-365°F. Cut approximately 50 parchment paper squares to 3"x3". Pipe a 2" doughnut-shaped circle onto one of the individual parchment squares.

4. Pipe the circles on each parchment until there is no more mixture (this might make a little more or a little less than 50 zeppoles, depending on how you pipe). Once everything is piped drop the first zeppole into the oil, parchment side up.

5. Allow it to fry until you just begin to see the edge turn a slight brown, then turn it over. Allow to fry for about 30 seconds then, using tongs, pull the parchment off the bottom of the zeppole and scoop the paper out of the oil, allowing it to continue to fry. It should cook for about 3 minutes in total; flip while frying to ensure even coloring. Continue to keep the oil between 355-365°F.

6. Pull the zeppole out of the oil and place onto a cooling rack to allow the oil to drain off. Dust with granulated sugar.

to serve:
Delicious with ricotta sorbet and chocolate sauce!

PENINSULA GRILL COCONUT CAKE

BY CLAIRE CHAPMAN

This cake is an original recipe from the beginning days of Peninsula Grill and is inspired by a coconut cake that was made by our original chef's grandmother. Over the years it has become synonymous with Peninsula Grill.

PENINSULA GRILL COCONUT CAKE

BY CLAIRE CHAPMAN

Serves 12-16

Preparation time: 2 hours
Cooking time: 45 minutes to an hour

ingredients

cake batter:

1 lb	butter
3 cups	sugar
6	eggs
4½ cups	flour
1½ cups	baking powder
½ tsp	salt
1½ cup	cream
1½ tbsp	vanilla extract
1 tsp	coconut oil

cake filling:

5 cups	cream
3 cups	granulated sugar
1 lb	unsalted butter
4 tbsp	cornstarch
1 tsp	vanilla extract
1 tbsp	water
9 cups	coconut, medium shred

frosting:

1 cup	butter, room temperature
8 oz	cream cheese
1 tsp	vanilla extract
1	vanilla bean, scraped
5 cups	powdered sugar
2 cups	coconut, toasted golden

simple syrup:

¾ cup	water
¾ cup	sugar

CHEF'S TIP

The cake is best when served at room temperature, but it is recommended to slice it while still cold.

method

cake batter:

Cream the butter and sugar together, then add the eggs one at time and mix until creamy. Sift the dry ingredients in a separate bowl. Mix the cream, vanilla and coconut extract together. Alternate the dry ingredients and wet ingredients into the batter and fill two 10" prepared cake pans evenly. Bake at 325°F until a toothpick comes out clean (about 45 minutes).

cake filling:

1. Boil the cream, sugar and butter together in a medium sauce pan. Mix the cornstarch, vanilla and water together to form a slurry. Slowly add the slurry to the boiling cream mixture, stirring constantly.
2. Bring to the boil and simmer for 1 minute. Remove from the heat and add the coconut. Let it cool over night. Just before assembling the cake, whip using the paddle attachment just until soft and creamy.

frosting:

Cream the butter and the cream cheese together. Add the vanilla, vanilla bean and powdered sugar and mix until creamy, white and smooth.

simple syrup:

Bring the water and sugar to a boil and then cool.

assembly:

Trim off the brown top from each sponge cake. Slice each cake into 3 layers horizontally and divide the filling into 5 even amounts. Starting with the first layer, brush with a ⅓ cup of the simple syrup. Spread a ⅕ of the filling evenly over the cake and continue with the remaining 5 cake layers, brushing each layer with simple syrup before spreading the filling.

to serve:

When all 6 layers are assembled, ice the cake with the frosting. Pat toasted coconut around the outside of the cake and chill for at least 5 hours. Cut into 12-16 pieces and serve with coconut crème Anglaise.

CHOCOLATE HAZELNUT CAKE WITH CARAMEL WHIPPED CREAM

BY ROBERT WENK

Now and again on a cold winter's evening when I am enjoying some leisure time at my log cabin in the beautiful Rockies, I crave something warm and chocolaty... here it is.

CHOCOLATE HAZELNUT CAKE WITH CARAMEL

BY ROBERT WENK

Serves 10

Preparation time: 30 minutes
Cooking time: 40-45 minutes

ingredients

chocolate hazelnut cake:

6 oz	bittersweet chocolate, cut into pieces
6 oz	butter
¼ cup	cake flour, sifted
1 tbsp	cocoa
¼ cup	coarsely chopped toasted hazelnuts
5	eggs, separated
½ tbsp	vanilla
¾ cup	sugar
pinch salt	

caramel whipped cream:

½ cup	sugar
2 cups	35% cream
2 tbsp	brandy

method

chocolate hazelnut cake:

1. Preheat the oven to 350°F.
2. In a double boiler over gently simmering water, melt the chocolate and butter stirring until smooth. Remove from the heat and cool slightly. In a small bowl, sift together the flour and cocoa. Stir in the hazelnuts and set aside.
3. Whisk together the egg yolks, vanilla and all but 2 tablespoons of the sugar until smooth and pale. Add the chocolate mixture, whisking slowly until smooth. Fold in the dry mixture.
4. In a separate bowl, beat the egg whites until the streaks hold and add the salt. Slowly add the rest of the sugar, beating until soft peaks form. Gently fold into the chocolate mixture.
5. Pour the batter into a 9" round springform pan lined with parchment paper. Bake on the middle rack for 40-45 minutes or until firm but still spongy in the middle. Set aside to cool completely on a wire rack. Note the cake will fall. Run a knife edge around the sides.

caramel whipped cream:

In a heavy bottom saucepan, heat the sugar until it is a caramel color. Remove from the heat and add a ½ cup of the 35% cream. Stand for 3 minutes until the bubbles subside. Add the brandy, stirring until combined. Set aside to cool – makes 1 cup. Whip the remaining 1½ cups of cream until firm peaks hold.

to serve:

Serve a slice of cake with a dollop of whipped cream and drizzled with caramel.

YOGURT PANNA COTTA WITH MIDDLETON FARM FRAISE DES BOIS

BY MICHAEL TUSK

 **At Ristorante Da Guido in Piemonte, I tasted my first panna cotta with fraise des bois and the panna cotta was heavenly.**

YOGURT PANNA COTTA WITH MIDDLETON FARM FRAISE DES BOIS

BY MICHAEL TUSK

Serves 4

Preparation time: 20 minutes
Planning ahead: This recipe can be done 8 hours ahead of serving or even the day before.
Specialist equipment: Silo design molds - The Silo Design Paris mold is the SD7XL

ingredients

yogurt panna cotta:

1 cup	yogurt
1¾ tbsp	granulated sugar
1¼	sheets of gelatin
½ cup	whipped crème fraîche

garnish:

½ cup	mixed varieties of fraise de bois

method

Heat half of the yogurt and sugar in a pot and mix until the sugar is dissolved. Add the bloomed gelatin. Strain the mixture over the second half of the yogurt mixture and then place onto an ice bath to cool while stirring constantly. Fold the yogurt mixture into the whipped crème fraîche and pour into large silo design molds and refrigerate until set.

to serve:

Remove the panna cotta from the refrigerator before serving and make a concentric circle of the berries, alternating the two varieties. Serve with freshly picked lemon verbena

CHEF'S TIP
This is not an un-molded panna cotta. Increase the gelatin if you would like to un-mold the panna cotta.

VANILLA BEAN BISCUITS WITH MINT & BASIL MACERATED STRAWBERRIES

BY JOSH DRAGE

Perfect for a summer cookout and the biscuit makes it very country.

VANILLA BEAN BISCUITS WITH MINT & BASIL MACERATED STRAWBERRIES

BY JOSH DRAGE

Serves 8-12

Preparation time: 30 minutes
Cooking time: 18 minutes

ingredients

biscuits:

1	vanilla bean
1⅓ cups	heavy cream
½ tsp	salt
4 tbsp	sugar
3 cup	flour
1 tbsp	baking powder
6 oz	butter
¼ cup	heavy cream

strawberries:

1 quartt 1 pt	strawberries
5	mint leaves
3	basil leaves
¼ cup	sugar
lemon juice	

method

biscuits:

1. Fillet the vanilla bean open and remove the inside with the back of the knife. Add to the 1⅓ cup of cream and stir in with a small whisk. Add the salt, sugar, flour and baking powder to a broad bowl. Whisk together.
2. Cut in the butter with a pastry knife until pea size. Mix into the 1⅓ cups cream with a fork. Before completely combined, pour out onto the counter and combine into a nice square. Roll out with a rolling pin to a 1" thickness.
3. Punch out with a biscuit cutter about ¾" or cut into squares. Brush the top of each biscuit with the remainder cream. Spread the biscuits out on a parchment lined baking sheet and bake at 350°F for about
18 minutes or until golden brown on top.

strawberries:

1. Remove the tops off of all the strawberries, quarter length wise and add to a mixing bowl. Rip the mint and basil leaves and add to the bowl. Add the sugar and lemon juice and macerate for 20 minutes. Remove a ⅓ of the strawberries and blend smooth.
2. Strain out the seeds with a basket strainer and add the sauce back to the strawberries.

to serve:

Cut the biscuits in ½. Put one half in a bowl, spoon over the strawberry sauce and add a spoon of whipped cream to the top of that. Top it with the other ½ of the biscuit, and fresh mint.

LEMON SEMIFREDDO

BY ERIC BAUER

A refreshing twist on a classic preparation, with the strawberry and rhubarb combination. Light and airy, this is a perfect dessert on a warm summer night or for someone who is trying to eat lightly.

LEMON SEMIFREDDO

BY ERIC BAUER

Serves 4-6

Preparation time: 24 hours
Cooking time: 20 minutes

ingredients

French meringue:
3	egg whites
3½ oz	powdered sugar
1 tsp	corn starch
3½ oz	granulated sugar

rhubarb jelly:
6½ oz	granulated sugar
32 oz	rhubarb purée
8	gelatin sheets, bloomed

lemon semi freddo:
3½ oz	granulated sugar
3	egg yolks
1½ oz	lemon juice
3	lemon zest
1	sheet gelatin
12 oz	whipped cream

method

French meringue:
Add all the ingredients into a mixer with paddle attachment and beat on a medium-high speed until very stiff peaks form and the meringue is smooth and not gritty to the touch between your finger tips. Place with an offset spatula onto a sheet tray lined with a silpat and cook at 200°F for approximately 15 minutes.

rhubarb jelly:
Bring the sugar and purée to a simmer. Bloom the gelatin by soaking in water for 2 minutes or until soft and pliable and add to the sugar mixture. Pour into a long form and cool to set. Cut out to the desired shape.

lemon semifreddo:
Whisk sugar and egg yolks until pale yellow. Add in the lemon juice and lemon zest. Bloom gelatin in water for 2-3 minutes. Heat up whipping cream until just simmering and pour the whipped cream over the yolk, sugar and lemon mixture. Add in the gelatin and place into desired forms. Freeze until very firm and set.

to serve:
Best served in individual portions cut 5"x1½" wide. Garnish with fresh berries and meringue.

IMAGE COURTESY OF MARTIN LEMIRE, MAGAZINE LE MUST

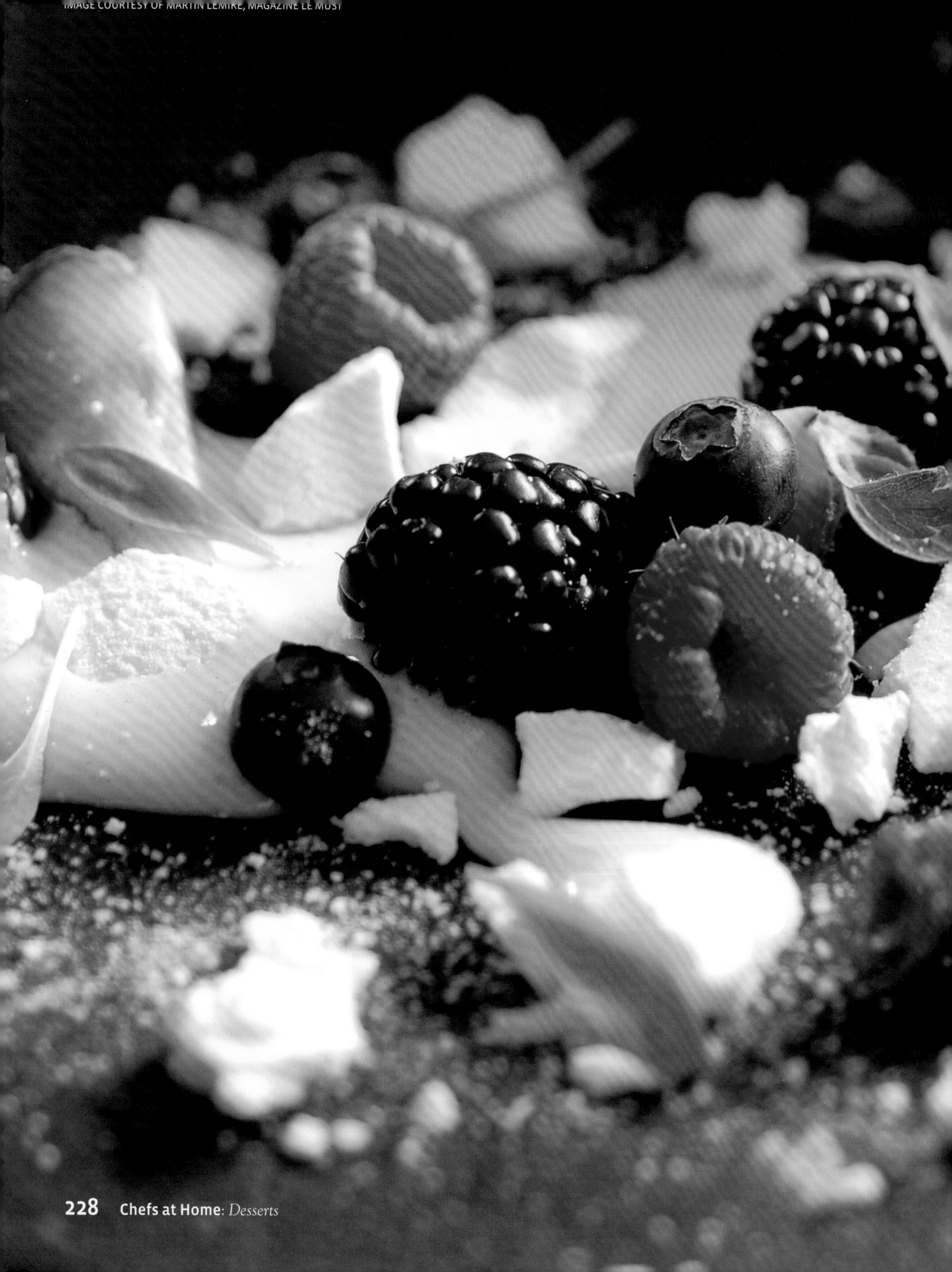

LITTLE RED BERRIES WITH CHAMPAGNE SABAYON

BY JEROME FERRER

 **Easy to make, pleasing to the eye and delightful for the palate. For your convenience, place the sabayon directly in the center of the table, or serve in individual pans.**

LITTLE RED BERRIES WITH CHAMPAGNE SABAYON

BY JEROME FERRER

Serves 4

Preparation time: 10 minutes
Cooking time: 10 minutes

ingredients

2 cups	mixed red berries
4	egg yolks
¼ cup	sugar
few drops	water
½ cup	dry Champagne
1 large	meringue, crushed
1 tbsp	coriander shoots

method

1. Wash the red fruits very well, drain and place in a large bowl.
2. In another large bowl, place the egg yolks, sugar and a few drops of water. Place the bowl over a pot of boiling water and whisk vigorously to make a sabayon (ribbon stage), gradually incorporating the Champagne.

to serve:
Spoon the smooth sabayon over the berries, sprinkle with a few meringue pieces and the coriander shoots. Place in the center of the table and share with good friends!

APPLES WITH CRISPY MAPLE BREAD, CRANBERRY SORBET, GREEN TOMATO CONFIT, YOGURT SAUCE, CIDER JELLY & CIDER CARAMEL

BY YVAN LEBRUN

Local produce is always high on the agenda for our dishes. These are simple ingredients but with this preparation they are transformed into something extraordinary.

APPLES WITH CRISPY MAPLE BREAD, CRANBERRY SORBET, GREEN TOMATO CONFIT, YOGURT SAUCE, CIDER JELLY & CIDER CARAMEL

BY YVAN LEBRUN

Serves 4

Preparation time: 1 hour
Cooking time: 2 hours

Special equipment: Ice cream maker

ingredients

apples:
4	Courtland apples
4 oz	butter
2 oz	maple syrup
2 oz	dry cider

crispy maple bread:
8 oz	sugar
2 oz	maple sugar
1	egg white
1 oz	hazelnut powder

cranberry sorbet:
2 cups	cranberry juice (natural and unsweetened)
¾ cup	sugar
1 cup	dried and ground cranberries
1 tsp	stabilizer

green tomato confit:
1 lb	green tomatoes, cubed
1	lemon, zest
8 oz	sugar

yogurt sauce:
1 cup	yogurt
2 tbsp	ice cider
	vanilla pod

spicy bread:
1	bay leaf
1	pinch each of salt, cinnamon, anise, ground cloves, pepper, cardamom, ginger
1	orange, zest
1 tbsp	yeast
3 oz	low flour
4 oz	spelt flour
3 oz	whole milk
1	egg, beaten
6 oz	honey

cider jelly:
1 cup	ice cider
4	leaves of gelatin

cider caramel:
	reserved apple juice
1 cup	35% cream

method

apples:
Preheat the oven to 275°F. Remove the apple cores then put the apples into a pan with the butter, maple syrup and cider. Place in the oven and cook for around 1 hour. Pour off the juice of the apples sometimes during cooking and reserve. Remove the apples from the oven and reserve.

crispy maple bread:
Preheat the oven to 300°F. Mix all the ingredients in a bowl. Spread on a silpat. Cook in the oven until it has a nice color, approximately 10 minutes.

cranberry sorbet:
Boil the cranberry juice with the sugar. Add the dried cranberries and the stabilizer. Mix and put in an ice cream maker.

green tomato confit:
Mix the green tomatoes with the zest of lemon and sugar. Cook in a pan until it is like a jam.

yogurt sauce:
Mix the yogurt with the ice cider and vanilla pod, and freeze.

spicy bread:
Preheat the oven to 300°F. Mix all the dry ingredients together then add the milk slowly, followed by the honey and egg. Cook in a nonstick cake pan for 30 minutes. Remove from the oven and let cool.

cider jelly:
Put the gelatin leaves in cold water to soften. Cook a quarter of the cider with the gelatin. Mix with the rest of the cider. Strain and pour into a bowl.

cider caramel:
Take the reserved apple juice and add the cream. Mix and cook, then keep warm.

to serve:
Break up the crispy maple bread into pieces and put onto four plates. Place an apple skin on each piece of crispy maple. Spoon around 1 teaspoon of green tomato confit. Add a cube of cider jelly, a touch of yogurt sauce and one quenelle of cranberry sorbet. Dip a cube of spicy bread in the caramel cider and add to the plate.

235

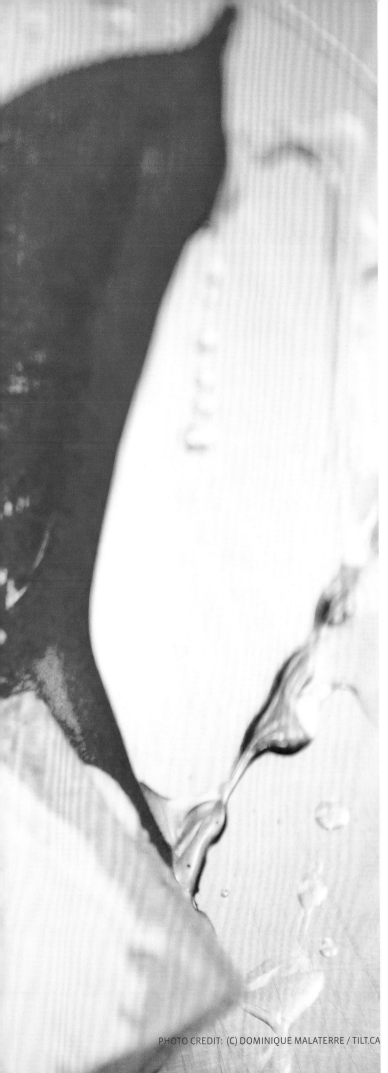

GIRLY CRANBERRIES

BY NORMAND LAPRISE

237

The kitchen brigade was playing around with a dacquoise, and the idea started from there. Then Charles-Antoine Crête, Chef de Cuisine, added cranberries and this gave the final idea.

GIRLY CRANBERRIES

BY NORMAND LAPRISE

Serves 4 to 6

Preparation time: 1½ hours
Cooking time: 1½ hours

ingredients

cranberry purée:
2 lb   cranberries
1 ½ cups   water
½ cup   sugar

cranberry sorbet:
½ cup   water
½ cup   sugar
cranberry pulp

cranberry syrup:
¼ cup   sugar

cranberry chips:
6   egg whites
1 cup   sugar

to serve:
¼ cup   thyme oil
½ cup   whipped cream
fresh thyme
Maldon salt
2 tbsp   dried olives, chopped

method

cranberry purée:
In a saucepan, over a medium heat, cook the cranberries with the water and sugar between 10-15 minutes, until all the fruits have burst. Pass through a sieve without pressing on the fruits too hard. Keep the water to make the syrup. Pass the pulp through a food processor and set aside to be used for both the chips and sorbet recipes.

cranberry sorbet:
1. In a saucepan, over a medium heat, cook the water and sugar together until the sugar is completely dissolved.
2. Mix 3 cups of the cranberry purée with a simple syrup made from sugar and water. Churn in an ice-cream maker according to manufacturer's instructions and rest in the freezer.

cranberry syrup:
In a saucepan, over medium heat, simmer the reserved cranberry water and sugar until the mixture has a syrupy consistency.

cranberry chips:
1. Preheat the oven to 225°F. Using a stand mixer, whisk the egg whites while gradually adding the sugar. Mix a quarter of this meringue with a ½ cup of the reserved cranberry purée. Using a spatula, delicately fold this mixture into the rest of the meringue. With a bent spatula, spread the meringue mixture a ¼" thick on a silicone baking mat. Separate it into four sectors by making a cross with the end of a wooden spoon. This will ensure that the cooking is uniform. Make sure that the 4 pieces made in this way do not touch each other.
2. Bake for 25 minutes. Turn the baking mat 180°F and cook for another 25 minutes. Flip the baking mat over on a baking sheet covered with parchment paper, remove the baking mat and cook another 25 minutes, until the meringue mixture is dry to the touch (your finger shouldn't leave a mark). Adjust the cooking time according to the texture of your mixture. The preparation should become crunchy after 5 minutes. Slice into 2" x 3" rectangles.

to serve:
1. On each plate, drizzle thyme oil and cranberry syrup. Place a scoop of sorbet. Stack 3 chips one over the other, and spread with whipped cream. Add thyme, Maldon salt and dried olives.
2. If you don't have thyme oil handy, make some in the following way:
3. In a saucepan filled with boiling water, blanch 3 cups of thyme leaves for 30 seconds. In a food processor, grind them quickly with 1 cup of grapeseed oil. Pour into a bowl and place this bowl in a second one filled with ice water to fix the preparation's colour. Leave it to infuse in the refrigerator for 4 hours.
4. Remove from the refrigerator and let the oil warm up to room temperature. Pass through a coffee filter and reserve.

LEMON-GLAZED BEIGNETS WITH HONEY-ROASTED ORGANIC HAZELNUTS

BY TERRY PICHOR

This recipe requires ingredients that can commonly be found in a home pantry. We originally started making beignets at the resort to use up excess brioche dough. We served them as morning pastries or with afternoon tea, and they were a huge hit. Beignets can be served at room temperature or hot from the fryer.

LEMON-GLAZED BEIGNETS WITH HONEY-ROASTED ORGANIC HAZELNUTS

BY TERRY PICHOR

Serves 12

Preparation time: 2 hours, +5 hours rising time
Cooking time: 1 hour, including frying, toasting and glazing
Special equipment: Deep-fry thermometer
Planning ahead:
Because of the long proofing time for the bread, I suggest starting this recipe in the early morning. Alternatively, start the night before and leave the dough in the refrigerator for the second proof. This will slow down the process so you can leave the dough until morning.

ingredients

brioche dough:

1 packet	active dry yeast
½ cup	warm water
2½ cups	all-purpose flour
2½ tsp	salt
⅓ cup	sugar
6	large eggs
1¼ cups	butter, cut into small pieces
all-purpose flour for dusting	
7 oz	brioche dough
canola oil	

honey-roasted hazelnuts::

2 tbsp	wildflower honey
2 tbsp	corn syrup
2 tbsp	granulated sugar
⅛ tsp	salt
2 cups	hazelnuts, chopped and toasted

lemon glaze:

zest and juice from 1 lemon	
1 cup	granulated sugar
½ cup	powdered sugar

method

brioche dough:

1. Add the yeast to the warm water and sit for 8-10 minutes. Stir well to dissolve. Set aside. Combine the flour, salt, sugar, eggs, and yeast mixture. With a dough hook attachment, mix on medium speed for 2-3 minutes until a sticky dough forms. At medium speed, add the butter in 3 stages, scraping the bowl each time until the butter is combined. Once all the butter has been added, increase the speed to high and mix until the dough ball forms around the dough hook, about 3 minutes.
2. Place the dough in a bowl and cover lightly with plastic wrap. Place in a warm dry place. Stand for 1½ hours, until the dough is twice its original volume.
3. Fold the dough 3-4 times to knock out the air. Cover again in plastic wrap and refrigerate for 5-6 hours while the dough rises.
4. About 2 hours before serving, weigh out 7 ounces of the dough for the beignets. The remaining dough can be frozen or baked into brioche.
5. Lightly flour a smooth, flat work surface. Roll the dough into a 2 foot long cylinder, about ½" in diameter. If the dough feels as if it will not stretch further, allow to rest for a few minutes, then roll again. Transfer to a cutting board and cover with a kitchen towel. Allow to rise until the dough looks soft and inflated, about 1-2 hours. Cut on the diagonal into 12 pieces, 2" long. Set aside.

honey-roasted hazelnuts:

1. Preheat the oven to 400°F. In a bowl, combine the honey, corn syrup, granulated sugar, and salt. Add the hazelnuts and toss to coat. Spread the hazelnuts in one layer on a parchment-lined baking sheet.
2. Bake the nuts until they start to bubble, stirring occasionally to disperse the glaze. The nuts are done when the glaze has thickened and the bubbles have slowed, about 15 minutes. Remove from the oven and cool completely on the tray. When the nuts are completely cool and dry, chop with a chef's knife.

lemon glaze:

Combine all the ingredients together. Set aside.

to serve:

1. In a heavy-bottomed pot, bring 3" of oil to 375°F on a deep fry thermometer. On the counter next to the stove, prepare a baking sheet with a wire rack over a layer of paper towels. One at a time, place the dough into the oil, moving and flipping it with a slotted spoon to ensure even cooking. When golden brown, carefully remove from the oil and rest on the rack. Repeat until all 12 beignets are cooked.
2. Set up the bowls of glaze and nuts. Dip each beignet in the glaze, then into the nuts. Toss until evenly coated. Repeat until all beignets are coated with nuts. Serve family-style.

THE FRENCH LAUNDRY
YOUNTVILLE, CALIFORNIA

CHOCOLATE PUDDING PIE

BY MILTON ABEL

245

 **Growing up, chocolate pudding pie was my dad's go-to dessert for the family so I wanted to replicate the memories of the dessert in an elevated way whilst maintaining the same elements all the way down to the Oreo cookie crust.**

CHOCOLATE PUDDING PIE

BY MILTON ABEL

Serves 4

Preparation time:	1½ hours
Cooking time:	1 hour

Special equipment: Kitchen Aid stand mixer, brûlée torch

Planning ahead: It is best to make the TKO crust and mousse ahead so that it can freeze overnight.

ingredients

TKO:

¾ cup + 1tbsp	sugar
1¾ cup + 1¾ tsp	flour
1 cup + 1½ tbsp	black cocoa powder
⅜ tsp	baking soda
2 tsp	salt
8 oz	cold butter

chocolate crémeux:

3½ oz	Guanaja 70% chocolate
10 oz	Jivara 40% milk chocolate
3 sheets	silver leaf gelatin
1¼ cup	heavy cream, to whip
⅓ cup	heavy cream
⅓ cup	whole milk
¼ cup	sugar
2	egg yolks

Swiss meringue:

7 oz	egg whites
1½ cups	sugar

method

TKO:

Mix together all the ingredients in a Kitchen Aid with a paddle attachment. Roll out the dough to a ¼" with a rolling pin and bake at 350°F for 15 minutes.

chocolate crémeux:

1. Mix the chocolates together over a double boiler and bloom the gelatin in cold water. Whip the 1¼ cup of cream to soft peaks. In a small pot combine the ⅓ cup of cream and whole milk and bring to a boil.
2. Mix together the sugar and egg yolks to incorporate. Remove the milk mixture from the heat and gradually add to the yolks while whisking continuously to temper. Add the mixture back into the original pot and continue to cook gently, stirring continuously, until it coats the back of a spoon. Add the bloomed gelatin to the Anglaise and cook until incorporated.
3. Pour the Anglaise over the melted chocolate and whisk to combine. Fold in the whipped cream.

Swiss meringue:

Whisk together the egg whites and sugar in a Kitchen Aid bowl over a bain marie. Once you can dip your finger into the mixture and it feels hot, remove the bowl from the heat. Place the bowl onto the Kitchen Aid stand mixer with the whisk attachment and whisk on high until the meringue is cool and stiff.

to serve:

Grind the baked TKO in a food processor to make small crumbs. Press the crumbs into the bottom of the cake ring to create about a ½" thick layer. Pour the crémeux over the top of the crust and freeze overnight. The next day, lightly heat the cake ring with a crème brûlée torch to remove the ring. Spread the Swiss meringue on the top and toast lightly with a crème brûlée torch. Serve as shown.

OLIVE OIL CAKE WITH BLUEBERRY COMPOTE & LEMON CURD

BY JIM GIOIA

The flavors of lemon and fruity olive oil make this a perfect summer dessert, when blueberries are in season.

OLIVE OIL CAKE WITH BLUEBERRY COMPOTE & LEMON CURD

BY JIM GIOIA

Serves 12

Preparation time: 45 minutes
Cooking time: 35-40 minutes

ingredients

cake:
5	eggs, separated
¾ cup	sugar
¾ cup	extra virgin olive oil
½	lemon, juice
1	lemon zest
1 cup	cake flour, sifted

blueberry compote:
2 pt	blueberries
½ cup	water
½ cup	sugar
3	strips of lemon zest

lemon curd:
6	eggs
2	egg yolks
2 cups	sugar
5	lemons, juice and zest
1 cup	cold butter, cubed

method

cake:
1. Grease and line with parchment a 9" round cake pan.
2. In the bottom of an electric mixer beat the egg whites with the whisk attachment on medium speed until light and frothy, about 1 minute. Gradually add ¼ cup sugar and continue whisking until soft peaks form. Transfer the whites to another bowl and set aside. Add the egg yolks to the empty mixing bowl and beat on medium speed with the paddle attachment and slowly add the remaining ½ cup of sugar, lemon juice and zest. Beat until lightened in color and thick.
3. With the mixer running, slowly drizzle in the olive oil in a steady stream. With the mixer on low speed add the flour, mixing until combined. Remove the bowl from the mixing stand. With a rubber spatula scrape the sides of the bowl and stir in a third of the egg whites to lighten the batter. Fold in the remaining egg whites in two additions, mixing gently until the mixture is combined. Pour into the prepared pan and bake at 350°F for 35-40 minutes. The top of the cake should just spring back when gently pressed.

blueberry compote:
Combine the sugar, zest and water in a medium saucepan and bring to a boil, dissolving the sugar. Cook for about 2 minutes until thick and then add the blueberries. Simmer gently until about half the blueberries begin to pop and the compote thickens. Pour into a bowl, remove the zest and chill..

lemon curd:
Combine all the ingredients, except the butter, in a mixing bowl. Place the bowl over a pot of simmering water and stir constantly with a wooden spoon, or a heat proof spatula until thick. Remove from the heat, stir in the butter, mixing until it is melted and combined. Pour the mixture through a sieve into a clean bowl, cover the surface with plastic wrap and chill.

to serve:
Swirl lemon curd on the plate. Add a slice of cake and top with a scoop of ice cream and blueberry compote.

STRAWBERRY & FRESH RHUBARB JELLY, WILD & FRESH STRAWBERRIES & CHANTILLY CREAM

BY MARK LEVY

 **Sun-warmed strawberries and cream has been a favorite of mine for a long time. Here is a great dinner party version of that dessert.**

STRAWBERRY & FRESH RHUBARB JELLY, WILD & FRESH STRAWBERRIES & CHANTILLY CREAM

BY MARK LEVY

Serves 4

Preparation time: 3 hours
Special equipment: 12 oz jello mold
Planning ahead: The jelly can be made up 2 days in advance.

ingredients

strawberry and rhubarb jelly:
6 oz	rhubarb concentrate
6 oz	fresh strawberry juice
4	gelatin leaves

strawberries:
16	ripe strawberries
16	wild strawberries
½	lemon, juiced
1 tsp	sugar
½	vanilla bean
1 cup	Chantilly cream

garnish:
¼ cup	rainbow sorrel leaves
10	blue borage flowers

method

strawberry and rhubarb jelly:
Gently warm the rhubarb concentrate and strawberry juice. Add and dissolve the bloomed gelatin sheets. Strain the liquid into the molds. Refrigerate for a minimum of 8 hours.

strawberries:
Meanwhile, hull and quarter the strawberries. Gently marinate in the lemon juice, sugar and vanilla. Reserve for later use.

to serve:
After 8 hours, turn the jelly out of the molds onto a chilled, circular serving dish. Decoratively arrange the marinated and wild strawberries around the outside. Top the jelly with a quenelle of Chantilly cream. Garnish with the flowers and herbs. Serve and enjoy!

CHEF'S TIP
The rhubarb concentrate adds an interesting flavor to the jelly, however the jelly can be made with only strawberry juice.

255

MEXICAN HOT CHOCOLATE WITH HOMEMADE MARSHMALLOWS

BY NOAH CARROLL

We make this rich, dark hot chocolate with traditional, crumbly Mexican chocolate tablets, perfect for warming up on a chilly day. Added here is a nostalgic American accent – homemade Graham crackers and marshmallows. They provide a touch more sweetness and layer of texture that pair perfectly with the lightly spiced, bittersweet brew.

MEXICAN HOT CHOCOLATE WITH HOMEMADE MARSHMALLOWS

BY NOAH CARROLL

Serves 8 - 10

Preparation time: 7 hours
Cooking time: 45 minutes

Special equipment: 8" x 8" baking pan, candy thermometer
Planning ahead: The honey marshmallows and Graham crackers can be made up to 3 days in advance.

ingredients

honey marshmallows:

1¹/₃ oz	gelatin sheets
2	cups caster sugar
½ cup	liquid glucose
¹/₃ cup	honey
1	vanilla bean, split and scraped
½ cup	powdered sugar
½ cup	cornstarch

Graham crackers:

4 tbsp	unsalted butter, at room temperature
1 tbsp	brown sugar
1 tbsp	caster sugar
1 tbsp	honey
¾ cup	all purpose flour
1 pinch	salt
1 pinch	baking soda
1 pinch	cinnamon powder

Mexican hot chocolate:

6 oz	(about 4 cups) Mexican chocolate, chopped
6 cups	milk

method

honey marshmallows:

1. Line an 8"x8" pan with greased wax paper. Soak the gelatin in ice water for 10 minutes; squeeze dry. Combine the caster sugar, glucose, honey and vanilla bean in a medium saucepan with a ¹/₃ cup of water. Using a candy thermometer, heat to 250°F. Strain the liquid through a fine meshed sieve into the bowl of an electric mixer. Cool at room temperature to 212°F and then add the gelatin sheets. Whip for 10 minutes, or until snowy white, thick and stiff. Pour into the prepared pan and smooth the top with an offset spatula. Rest at room temperature for at least 6 hours to set.

2. Combine the powdered sugar and cornstarch in a large mixing bowl. Dust a cutting board with half of the sugar/cornstarch mixture and turn the marshmallow onto the board - peel and discard the wax paper. Cut to desired shapes and toss in the remaining sugar mixture to coat and prevent sticking. Store in an airtight container. If desired, toast some of the marshmallows over an open flame before serving.

Graham crackers:

1. In the bowl of an electric mixer fitted with a paddle attachment, mix the butter, brown sugar, caster sugar and honey until fluffy. Combine and sift together the flour, salt, baking soda and cinnamon and incorporate into the butter mixture. Mix on a low speed until well combined. Line a flat surface with a sheet of wax paper and scrape the dough on top. Top with another sheet of wax paper and with a rolling pin, roll out to an approximately 9½" wide x 13" long x 3mm thick rectangle. Transfer to a baking sheet and place in a freezer until solid.

2. Preheat the oven to 350°F. Line a baking sheet with parchment paper. Working quickly, cut the frozen dough into 1"x5" rectangles and transfer to the prepared baking sheet. Bake for 8-10 minutes, or until the edges of the crackers are browned. Cool at room temperature and store in an airtight container.

Mexican hot chocolate:

Place the chocolate into a heat proof bowl. Pour the milk into a saucepan and bring to a simmer. Pour over the chocolate and purée with a hand blender until smooth.

to serve:

Divide the hot chocolate into coffee mugs and serve with Graham crackers and honey marshmallows as shown.

KEY LIME CHEESECAKE WITH BERRY COMPOTE

BY GIANCARLO D'ATTILI, PASTRY CHEF

This is an all-American dessert with a twist of bright key lime juice.

KEY LIME CHEESECAKE WITH BERRY COMPOTE

BY GIANCARLO D'ATTILI, PASTRY CHEF

Serves 16

Preparation time: 45-60 minutes

ingredients

Graham cracker crust:

2 cups	Graham cracker crumbs
1	pinch kosher salt
1 cup	melted butter

key lime cheesecake:

14 oz	granulated sugar
½ tsp	kosher salt
¾ oz	cornstarch
2½ lb	cream cheese, room temperature
8 oz	eggs
4 oz	egg yolks
2 oz	whole milk
2 oz	heavy cream
juice	5 key limes
zest	1 key lime

berry compote:

8 oz	strawberries, quartered
½ cup	granulated sugar
¼ cup + 4 tbsp	cold water
2 tbsp	cornstarch
4 oz	raspberries
4 oz	blackberries
4 oz	blueberries

method

Graham cracker crust:

Combine the crumbs with the salt in a bowl. Add the melted butter and mix until combined. Press into a 10" ring or spring-form pan.

key lime cheesecake:

1. Combine the sugar and salt with the cornstarch. Mix into the cream cheese.
2. Combine the eggs with the egg yolks and add to the mix, in stages. Add the milk, cream, and lime juice. Strain the mix to avoid any lumps. Add the lime zest. Pour into the crust-lined ring or spring-form pan and place in a water bath. Bake at 300°F until set, about 45-60 minutes. Allow to completely cool before unmolding from the ring/spring-form pan.

berry compote:

1. In a sauce pot, place the strawberries, sugar, and water. Mix the cornstarch with about 4 tablespoons of water and set aside. Bring the strawberries to the boil and add the cornstarch mix. Cook over a low heat for 2 minutes, or until the mix thickens and the starch flavor has been cooked off.
2. Remove from the heat and add the rest of the berries. Cool to room temperature and pour over the cooled cheesecake.

to serve:
Slice and enjoy!

BANANA CAKE

BY TROY HIMMELMAN

Bananas are a great ingredient to always have on hand. They are easily used in all aspects of the kitchen from breakfast, lunch, packed lunches for horse back rides and dinner as well.

BANANA CAKE

BY TROY HIMMELMAN

Serves 24

Preparation time: 1 hour 40 minutes
Cooking time: 1 hour

ingredients

banana cake:
11 oz	sugar
4¾ oz	shortening
4 ea	bananas
1lb 3½ oz	all-purpose flour
½ oz	baking powder
¼ oz	baking soda
¼ oz	salt
1 pint	buttermilk
1 tsp	vanilla extract
¾ cup	walnut
¾ cup	milk chocolate shavings

ice cream base:
1 quart	heavy cream
1¼ cup	milk
9¼ oz	sugar
7 oz	egg yolks

caramel:
8 oz	heavy cream
8 oz	granulated sugar
2 oz	water

tuile:
2 ½ oz	butter, soft
3 ½ oz	powdered sugar
2 ½ oz	honey
3 ½ oz	all-purpose flour
2 ea	egg whites

blackberry coulis:
12 oz	frozen blackberries
4 oz	sugar
1 tsp	vanilla extract
2 oz	water
1 oz	cornstarch

to serve:
candied Macadamia nuts of your choice
gianduja (hazelnut chocolate bar)

method

banana cake:
1. Combine the sugar and shortening in a standing mixer with the paddle attachment and cream until light and fluffy. Add the bananas and blend until large pieces are no longer prevalent. Sift the flour, baking powder, baking soda and salt together and add them into the bowl alternating with the buttermilk. Blend until almost fully combined. Fold in the walnuts and milk chocolate shavings
2. Fill flexi pan molds about half full with the batter and bake at 350°F for approximately 15 minutes in a convection oven.
3. Remove from the oven and immediately flip the pan onto another sheet pan lined with parchment paper to cool and level the tops which are now the bottoms.
4. Once cooled remove from the molds and cover with plastic wrap.
5. Can be refrigerated for up to 2 days covered.

ice cream base:
1. Combine the heavy cream, milk and ½ the sugar in a 2 quart heavy bottom saucepot.
2. Bring to a boil and temper in the combined yolks and second ½ of the sugar.
3. Cook to a nappe and strain into a metal bain-marie set in an ice bath to cool to 40°F
4. Churn in an ice cream machine according to manufacturer's instructions.

caramel:
1. Heat the heavy cream in a separate container, bringing to a boil and reserve.
2. Combine the sugar and water in a heavy bottomed sauce pan and bring to a boil.
3. Wash down the sides of the pot with a pastry brush and cook to an amber colored caramel.

4. Pour the heavy cream into the caramel off the flame a little at a time being careful since the caramel will boil up and steam will be released. Continue to add the cream until all is added. Return to flame and stir together until the caramel is fully combined Strain into a container and cool.

tuile:
1. Cream the butter, sugar, honey and flour and then slowly add the egg whites. Spoon onto a silpat and bake at 350°F until golden brown
2. Remove from the oven and while slightly warm remove from the silpat and place onto parchment paper to cool. Place in a container and wrap airtight.

blackberry coulis:
1. Combine the blackberries, sugar and vanilla extract in a heavy bottomed saucepan and slowly bring to a boil. Simmer slowly for about 5 minutes and strain the liquid into another pot. Bring back to a boil and skim off all the excess foam to make a clear liquid. Once all the foam has been skimmed off, combine the water and cornstarch and add slowly while whisking into the jus until the consistency is correct for a sauce.
2. Strain and cool covered so as not to form a skin.

to serve:
1. Crush some of the candied macadamia nuts and fold into the ice cream base along with the caramel. You will probably not need all the caramel so reserve some for another use.
2. Decorate the plate with the blackberry sauce. Place a banana cake on the plate, then the tuile on top and next a quenelle of ice cream on top.
3. Shave the gianduja with a peeler and place curls on top of the ice cream.
4. Enjoy!

267

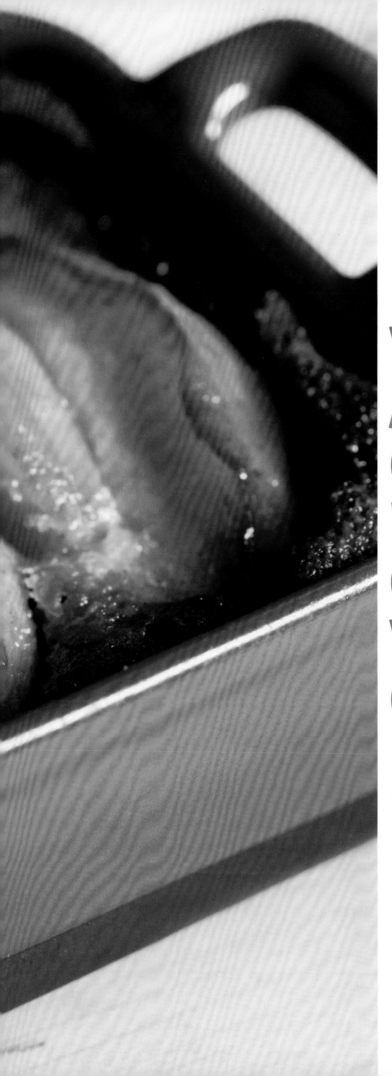

VERMONT APPLE CLAFOUTIS WITH WILD GINGER & VANILLA GELATO FLOAT

BY CHRISTOPHER WILSON

This dish is a celebration of our local apple harvest and done in a slightly different version each and every year. This year, at Twin Farms, it is served with a wild crafted ginger beer float. This clean and simple ginger float seemed a great way to showcase its flavor without being too overpowering.

VERMONT APPLE CLAFOUTIS WITH WILD GINGER & VANILLA GELATO FLOAT

BY CHRISTOPHER WILSON

Serves 6

Preparation time:	1 hour 45 minutes
Cooking time:	45 minutes
Special equipment:	Carbonation machine

Planning ahead: This dish may be prepared just prior to baking up to 2 days in advance, then baked as needed.

ingredients

Vermont Crispin apple clafoutis:

5	crispin apples or equivalent
4 tbsp	butter
2 oz	Vermont apple brandy
6 oz	organic granulated sugar
1 tsp	Ceylon cinnamon
½ tsp	ground ginger
½ tsp	kosher salt

custard:

3	eggs at room temperature
1 cup	milk
1 tsp	vanilla extract
1 tsp	kosher salt
½ cup	pastry flour (or gluten free)
⅓ cup	gluten free bread flour blend
1½ tsp	xanthan gum

wildcrafted ginger float:

8 pieces	wild crafted ginger root, 6" long
2 cups	organic granulated sugar
2 cups	water
1 liter	home carbonated or purchased carbonated water

to serve:

Fine maple sugar

CHEF'S TIP

This Apple Clafoutis may also be prepared Gluten Free: combine a ⅓ cup of white rice flour, 3 tablespoons of tapioca flour, 3 tablespoons of potato starch and 1½ teaspoons xanthan gum and substitute that for the pastry flour in the recipe. There is nothing like the flavor of wild ginger, but if you do not have a source for it, or can not responsibly wild craft it, a craft ginger beverage would work as well, like Maine root ginger beer.

method

apples:

1. Peel, core and 12-cut the apples into wedges. In a large sauté pan on a high heat, toast the butter until frothy and almost browned. Add the apples and sauté briefly, try to get a bit of color on the fruit. Deglaze with the brandy, whisk together the sugar and spices, sprinkle on top of the fruit and gently stir in.
2. Allow the mixture to come to a boil, but be sure not to cook the apples more than 70% through. Strain the apple mixture through a coarse strainer, reserving the syrup for the custard.

custard:

Place the eggs, milk and vanilla in a pitcher or bowl with an immersion blender. Blend the liquids, adding the dry ingredients a handful at a time. When incorporated, stream in the warm syrup from the sautéed apples and allow to rest for 10 minutes.

wildcrafted ginger float:

1. Wash, peel by scraping the skin off and mince the root. Bring the sugar and water to a boil, add the wild ginger root and allow to cool to room temperature.
2. Strain out the ginger and refrigerate until cold. Add a ½ cup of ginger syrup to 1 liter of carbonated water. Scoop the homemade vanilla bean gelato into mugs and top with wild ginger soda, some of the additional syrup can be drizzled on top for an extra kick.

to serve:

1. Place 8-10 apple wedges into each vessel, they do not need to be flat, the custard should work between the pieces. Cover with batter (approximately a 4 ounce ladle into a red roaster) this could also be done in a larger 9" pie plate.
2. When all are portioned, sprinkle the tops with a generous amount of fine maple sugar to help to create a thin crust. Bake in a convection at 375ºF or a still oven at 400ºF until they souffle' nicely, are crusty and deep golden brown. This should be approximately 30-45 minutes depending on your oven.
3. Serve immediately, or hold warm until needed.

EGGNOG JELLO

BY MAURICIO NAVARRO SPAMER

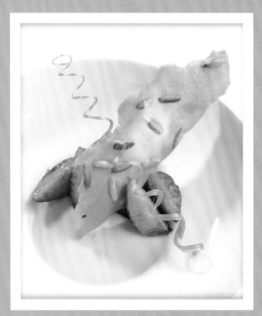

In Mexico eggnog (rompope) is a popular beverage. Here you find a mixture of French, Spanish and Mexican creativity. It reminds us of our cultural heritage.

EGGNOG JELLO

BY MAURICIO NAVARRO SPAMER

Serves 10

Preparation time: 2 hours
Cooking time: 10 minutes

ingredients

eggnog jello:

3 tbsp	gelatin
1 cup	water
2 cups	milk
1 ½ cups	eggnog
7oz	condensed milk

pumpkin seed tuiles:

⅓ cup	flour
½ cup	granulated sugar
2 tbsp	granulated sugar
¼ cup	pumpkin seeds
1 pinch	salt
3 egg	whites
5 tbsp	unsalted butter
milk, as needed	

strawberries with balsamic vinegar:

2 cups	strawberries
3 tbsp	balsamic vinegar

to serve:

3 tbsp	sugar

method

eggnog jello:
Dissolve the gelatin in the water. Blend the milk, eggnog and condensed milk together. Add to the gelatin and mix together. Strain if necessary and then refrigerate for 2 hours.

pumpkin seed tuiles:
1. Sift the flour, sugar, pumpkin seeds and salt into a small mixing bowl. Add the egg whites and then the melted unsalted butter, and whisk until just combined. Set the batter aside to rest for 1 ½ hours before using, or cover and refrigerate for up to 3 days. Preheat the oven to 350°F. Heavily butter some parchment paper, and place on 3 baking sheets. Using ½ a tablespoon per tuile, spoon the batter onto the baking sheets, 5 per sheet. The cookies should be at least 2" apart, as they spread during baking. Dipping a finger in the milk first, spread each cookie into a 3" round. To insure even baking, make the edges no thinner than the centers.
2. Bake the tuiles 8-10 minutes or until the edges are golden and the centers are just beginning to color. Remove the cookies from the oven. As soon as they are cool enough to handle, remove the tuiles from the baking sheets and drape them around rolling pins or wine bottles. If the cookies become too cool and stiff to bend, return them to the oven for a minute or so and they will soften up.

strawberries with balsamic vinegar:
In a large bowl place strawberries and drizzle with balsamic.

to serve:
Allow to sit at room temperature for up to 30 minutes.
Sprinkle with sugar.

BAKED LEMON PUDDING WITH SOUR CREAM CUSTARD, BLUEBERRY & PORT COMPOTE

BY LEE PARSONS

A light summer lemon dessert accompanied with locally grown Chandler blueberries

BAKED LEMON PUDDING WITH SOUR CREAM CUSTARD, BLUEBERRY & PORT COMPOTE

BY LEE PARSONS

Serves 8

Preparation time: 30 minutes
Cooking time: 25 minutes

ingredients

lemon pudding:

1 tbsp	grated lemon zest
6 tbsp	lemon juice
3 large	eggs separated
1½ cups	2% milk
6 tbsp	plain flour
1½ cups	white granulated sugar
1 pinch	salt
3 large	eggs separated

sour cream custard:

1	vanilla pod
2 cups	milk
1 cup	sour cream
8	egg yolks
3oz	caster sugar
½ tsp	cornstarch

blueberry and port compote:

1lb	blueberries
3 1/2 fl oz	ruby port
3 oz	sugar
2 fl oz	lemon juice
5	basil leaves
10	mint leaves

method

lemon pudding:

1. Whisk together the sugar, lemon zest, lemon juice and the egg yolks. Add the milk and salt and fold in the flour to form a smooth mixture.
1. In a separate bowl beat the egg whites until stiff and glossy. Fold the beaten egg whites into the lemon mixture. Pour the batter into 8 greased #1 ramekins, place these into a larger pan and add water to come half way up the sides. Bake at 350°F for 25 minutes or until golden on top.

sour cream custard:

1. Split and scrape the vanilla pod. Add the split pod to the milk and cream and bring to the boil.
2. Whisk together the egg yolks, sugar and cornstarch in a bowl until smooth.
3. Scald the egg mix with a ⅓ of the boiled milk. Add the remaining milk and cook until the mix has reached the ribbon stage, stirring constantly. (If the custard mix splits, cool slightly and hand blend until smooth.) Pass the mix through a fine strainer, chill and reserve.

blueberry and port compote:

Place ½ of the blueberries, ruby port, sugar and lemon juice into a pan and simmer for 10 minutes. Add the basil and mint and infuse for 10 minutes. Pass the blueberry purée through a fine strainer. Add the remaining berries and chill.

to serve:

1. Spoon 2 table spoons of the sour cream custard into a shallow bowl. Carefully turn the puddings out and place in the center of the bowl.
2. Spoon the blueberry compote around base of the lemon pudding and finish with a dusting of icing sugar and mint sprig before serving.

PEACH COBBLER WITH BOURBON CHANTILLY CREAM

BY NATE CURTIS

This is a nice, easy and delicious dessert. Handed down from my wife's grandmother, it's a family favorite.

PEACH COBBLER WITH BOURBON CHANTILLY CREAM

BY NATE CURTIS

Serves 8

Preparation time: 30 minutes
Cooking time: 45 minutes

ingredients

Chantilly cream:

¼ cup	Bourbon
¼ cup	brown sugar
1 cup	heavy cream

cobbler:

½ cup	butter
1 cup	all-purpose flour
1 cup	white granulated sugar (plus 2 tbsp for dusting the top of the cobbler)
1½ tsp	baking powder
⅔ cup	whole milk
1 lb	peaches (sliced or use a 1 lb can sliced peaches)

to serve:
blackberries

method

Chantilly cream:
Combine the Bourbon and the sugar in a saucepan and cook for 15 minutes over a low heat until completely incorporated. Whisk with the cream until soft peaks form. Reserve.

cobbler:
Preheat the oven to 300°F. Melt the butter in an 8"x8" baking dish. Mix the flour, sugar, baking powder and milk together. Pour the flour mixture into the middle of the baking dish. Place the peaches in the middle. Dust the top of the cobbler with sugar. Bake for 45 minutes.

to serve:
Spoon out the cobbler and top with the whipped cream and blackberries.

MAINE BLUEBERRY CRUMBLE WITH VANILLA CREAM

BY JONATHAN CARTWRIGHT

My favorite home dessert, my children love to pick blueberries for this and love to taste the fruits of their labor.

MAINE BLUEBERRY CRUMBLE WITH VANILLA CREAM

BY JONATHAN CARTWRIGHT

Serves 8

Preparation time: 20 minutes
Cooking time: 45 minutes

ingredients

2 lbs	wild Maine blueberry, flash frozen wild Maine blueberries can also be used
2 lbs	caster sugar
2 tsp	lemon juice
½ lb	unsalted Maine butter
1 lb	cake flour
1	vanilla bean
½ quart	whipping cream

method

1. Mix the cleaned washed blueberries with 1 pound of the sugar and the lemon juice and cook in a sauce pan over a medium heat for 20 minutes until the juices are thick and blueberries are a chewy jam consistency.
2. Line the bottom of an appropriate sized oven proof dish with the cooked blueberries.
3. Crumble the cold butter, the remaining sugar and flour in a bowl until it resembles bread crumbs; cover the top of the blueberries with the crumble mix.
4. Place the dish in a preheated oven at 350°F for 35 to 45 minutes or until the crust is golden brown.
5. In the mean time, split the vanilla bean and scrape the seeds into the cream in a bowl. Whip the cream and vanilla until it reaches medium peaks. Sugar may also be added to this but I prefer to have no sugar in the cream as the blueberry crumble is sweetened.

CHOCOLATE TART WITH MANDARIN & BEETS

BY MATT WILSON

The inspiration for this dish comes from the marriage of the flavors of fall and chocolate. The earthiness of the beets goes really well with dark chocolate and the mandarin adds a refreshing citrus component.

CHOCOLATE TART WITH MANDARIN AND BEETS

BY MATT WILSON

Serves 4

Preparation time: 1½ hours
Cooking time: 30 minutes

ingredients

chocolate tart:
½ cup	36% cream
½ cup	homogenized milk
¾ cup	64% chocolate
1	egg

sorbet syrup:
1²/₃ cup	sugar
1¾ cup	water
2 tbsp	liquid glucose

mandarin sorbet:
3 cups	mandarin purée
1¹/₃ cups	sorbet syrup
1	lemon, juiced

beet purée:
1 cup	red beets, peeled and diced
¹/₃ cup	sorbet syrup
1	lemon, juiced

sable dough:
2 cups	all purpose flour
²/₃ cup	butter
1 cup	icing sugar
2	egg yolks
1 pinch	salt

method

chocolate tart:
1. Place the cream and milk into a pan and bring to the boil and place the chocolate into a heat proof bowl. Once the milk and cream has come to the boil, pour over the chocolate and mix until all the chocolate has melted. Add the egg to this mixture whilst mixing so that it does not cook the egg straight away.
2. Place the chocolate mixture back into the pan and heat, stirring constantly until the mixture reaches 185°F. Take the mixture off the heat and strain through a fine mesh strainer. Place into either pastry shells or place into pre-prepared metal rings.

mandarin syrup:
Place all the ingredients into a pan and bring to the boil for 2 minutes, then remove from the heat and cool. Reserve until needed in the sorbet recipe.

mandarin sorbet:
Mix all the ingredients together until combined and churn in an ice cream machine according to manufacturer's instructions. Churn until you able to scoop the sorbet.

beet purée:
Place all the ingredients in a vacuum sealed bag in boiling water until they are soft. Place the entire contents in a blender whilst still hot, blend until smooth then place in a container and cover the surface with plastic wrap so a skin does not form on top and cool in an ice bath.

sable dough:
1. Place the flour, butter, icing sugar and the salt in an electric mixing bowl and using the paddle attachment, mix until resembles bread crumbs. Add the yolks and mix until just combined. Take the dough out of the machine and work lightly on a bench until the dough looks combined and smooth. Allow the dough to rest in the fridge for an hour.
2. After resting, roll out the dough until it is roughly a ¼" thick and then you can either line a conventional tart mold or bake the sheet of pastry until is three quarter cooked, then cut out rings that the same size as the chocolate tart. Continue baking until golden brown around the edges bake in a 400°F oven for approximately 10-15 minutes.

to serve:
Place a spoonful of the beet purée on the plate and using a small palette knife smear the purée over the plate. If you have placed the chocolate mix into the metal rings you will need to heat the outside of the ring to release the tart. Once released place the chocolate tart on top of the sable disc then place in the center of the beet smear. Make a quenelle out if the mandarin sorbet and place on top of the chocolate tart and serve.

WINDHAM HILL BAKED ALASKA

BY GRAHAM GILL

 This is a classic Baked Alaska with a twist. Local berries are served around the Baked Alaska

WINDHAM HILL BAKED ALASKA

BY GRAHAM GILL

Serves 4

Preparation time: 2 hours
Cooking time: 5 minutes
Special equipment: Electric mixer

ingredients

sponge:

¹/₃ cup	vegetable oil
4	egg yolks
½ cup	water at room temperature
½ tbsp	vanilla extract
7 oz	cake flour
7 oz	granulated sugar
2 tsp	baking powder
½ tsp	salt
4	egg whites

ice cream:

1 cup	sugar
8	egg yolks
1½ cups	milk
½ cup	heavy cream
1 cup	fresh local strawberries, diced

meringue:

2	egg whites
4 oz	sugar

method

sponge:

1. Line 1 square 12"x12" cake tin with baking paper. Whip the vegetable oil and egg yolks together just until combined. Stir in the water and vanilla extract. Sift together the cake flour, ¹/₃ of the sugar, the baking powder and the salt. Stir this into the egg yolk mixture and then whip at high speed for 1 minute.

2. Whip the egg whites to a foam. Gradually add the remaining sugar and continue whipping until stiff peaks form. Carefully fold the meringue into the batter and pour into the prepared cake tin. Bake at 375ºF for approximately 25 minutes or until the cake springs back when pressed lightly in the center. Invert the pans on a rack and allow the cakes to cool in the pans before un-molding.

ice cream:

Whisk the sugar and eggs together. Bring the milk and heavy cream to a boil, add half of the liquid to the egg mixture, whisk and add back to the pot with the remaining liquid to cook on a low heat until it coats the back of a spoon. Cool and then add the strawberries. Churn in an ice cream maker according to manufacturer's instructions and place in the freezer until firm.

meringue:

Whisk the egg whites to stiff peaks, add the sugar slowly.

to serve:

Cut out a 2" circle of sponge. Place on an oven safe tray. Place a scoop of ice cream on top and then pipe the meringue to completely cover the sponge and ice cream. Place in a 450ºF oven for 2 minutes until it has a little color. Serve with fresh berries around the outside and a sprig of mint leaf.

TRIO OF COOKIES

BY GILLES BALLAY

Cookies – always a favorite with adults and children alike. There is something for everyone with the choice of chocolate, peanut butter or oatmeal.

TRIO OF COOKIES

BY GILLES BALLAY

makes approximately 50 cookies each

Cooking time: 12-15 minutes

ingredients

cherry chocolate oatmeal cookies:

6 tsp	melted butter
¾ cup	brown sugar
1	egg
1 tsp	vanilla extract
⅓ cup	all purpose flour
⅓ cup	wheat flour
1½ cups	old fashioned oats
3 oz	semi-sweet chocolate
1 cup	dry cherries
½ tsp	salt
1 tsp	baking soda

peanut butter cookies:

8 oz	butter
8 oz	sugar
6 oz	brown sugar
2	eggs
few drops	vanilla extract
8 oz	chunky peanut butter
13 oz	all purpose flour
1 pinch	salt
½ oz	baking powder
4 oz	salted peanuts

caramelized nuts of choice as well as a few chunks of gianduja to place on top of the cookies (optional)

chocolate dream cookies:

8 oz	unsweetened chocolate
1½ lb	sweet dark chocolate chips
6 oz	butter
11½ oz	all purpose flour
1 pinch	baking powder
1 pinch	salt
8	eggs
1½ lb	sugar
½ oz	instant espresso powder
1 oz	vanilla extract
1½ lb	chocolate chips

method

cherry chocolate oatmeal cookies:

1. Preheat the oven to 350°F low fan. Mix the butter with the sugar. Add the egg and vanilla extract then add the rest of the ingredients.
2. Keep the dough in the refrigerator for at least 15 minutes. Place scoops of the dough on a parchment-lined cookie sheet and bake for approximately 12 minutes depending on size.

peanut butter cookies:

1. Preheat the oven to 325°F low fan. Using a mixer with a paddle attachment, cream the butter and sugars. Add the eggs and vanilla extract, then add the peanut butter.
2. Add all the dry ingredients to make a dough. Scoop balls of desired size onto a cookie sheet lined with buttered parchment paper.
3. Bake in the oven for approximately 12 minutes or until cooked.
4. Place the caramelized nuts and gianduja decoratively on the cookies while they are still hot.

chocolate dream cookies:

1. Preheat the oven to 325°F low fan. Melt the unsweetened chocolate, sweet dark chocolate chips, and butter together. Mix the flour, baking powder and salt in a separate bowl. Using a mixer with a paddle attachment, beat the eggs, sugar, espresso powder, and vanilla extract until light. Add the chocolate/butter mixture at low speed.
2. In increments add the flour mix to the egg/chocolate mixture until combined. Stir in the chocolate chips.
3. Allow the mixture to fully cool then scoop desired-sized balls onto buttered parchment on a cookie sheet.
4. Bake for approximately 12-15 minutes or until cooked.

to serve:

Allow the cookies to cool to room temperature or serve warm.

CHEF'S TIP
Cookie dough can be made and frozen in advance.

ADDISON

AUBERGE DU SOLEIL

AUBERGE SAINT-ANTOINE

At Addison, The Grand Del Mar's signature restaurant, Director and Executive Chef William Bradley's artisanal approach to cooking, based on his admiration for French cuisine, draws inspiration from the seasons and California's bounty.

Addison's Mediterranean décor, which echoes the design of the world-class The Grand Del Mar resort, is an elegant backdrop to chef Bradley's multi-course seasonal tasting menus. Impeccable service and an award-winning wine program that also offers exclusive proprietary wine bottlings, complete the dining experience at Addison. Addison's Le Grand Table provides guests with an intimate, behind-the-scenes dining experience personally presided over by Chef Bradley. He works directly with the guest host to customize a one-of-a-kind tasting menu with wine pairings for each course created by Addison's esteemed sommeliers.

French restaurateur Claude Rouas has created a discreet and elegant hotel hidden among a grove of olive trees that evoke his love of Provence in the South of France.

Situated at the heart of the Cabernet-Sauvignon, Merlot and Chardonnay vines of Napa Valley, the 15,000 bottle wine cellar promises an oenophile's journey to wine heaven as you watch the sun set on the horizon. A handful of cottages perched on the hillside offer spacious 'maisons' with private terraces where aged French oak floors, colorful chenille fabrics, abstract paintings and fireplaces create an air of romance. The Mediterranean-inspired cuisine features the very best of the region. The spa which also draws its cue from the land, proposes treatments based on grapes, olives, herbs, flowers, mud and minerals.

With its irresistible charm and gourmet cuisine, the Auberge Saint-Antoine is nestled in the heart of Québec, the first city to be founded in North America.

"The impression made upon the visitor by this Gibraltar of America: its giddy heights, its citadel suspended, as it were in the air, its picturesque steep streets and frowning gateways, and the splendid views which burst upon the eye at every turn, is at once unique and lasting ...," wrote Charles Dickens on the subject of Québec city. The Auberge Saint-Antoine is a perfect place to stay to share in the writer's wonderment. This Vieux-Port hotel stands on a unique archaeological site. When it was built, many relics from French and English colonial times were discovered. Today, they adorn the chic, wood and cast iron designer interiors of this museum location.

ADDISON

5200 Grand Del Mar Way
San Diego, California 92130
United States
Tel.: + 1 858 314 1900
Fax: + 1 858 314 1920
E-mail: addison@relais.com
Website: www.relais.com/addison

AUBERGE DU SOLEIL

180 Rutherford Hill Road
Rutherford, California 94573
United States
Tel.: + 1 707 963 1211
Fax: + 1 707 963 8764
E-mail: soleil@relais.com
Website: www.relais.com/soleil

AUBERGE SAINT-ANTOINE

8 rue Saint-Antoine
Québec, Québec G1K 4C9
Canada
Tel.: + 1 888 692 2211
Fax: + 1 418 692 1177
E-mail: antoine@relais.com
Website: www.relais.com/antoine

BEDFORD POST INN

Offering an elegant, intimate experience in one of the most charming parts of New York.

A fourteen-acre retreat located just under one hour north of New York City in the hamlet of Bedford, is home to an eight-room luxury inn, two distinct restaurants and a yoga studio. Understated elegance and warm, gracious hospitality are Bedford Post hallmarks that make it the perfect escape. Built in the early 1760s in Dutch Colonial style, Bedford Post is one of only three original structures from the 18th century that remains in Bedford today.

BLACKBERRY FARM

This traditional farm is deep in Tennessee and offers a chance to return to nature and rediscover life's simple pleasures. Guests are treated to a steady flow of deliciously fresh produce all year round as part of the 1700 hectares of land set aside for farming.

In addition to vegetables, cheese, herbs, honey, cider and much more are all produced right here. Established ties with local gardeners and tradespeople mean that Blackberry Farm's team of Chefs offers a menu that respects the authenticity of the flavors and the integrity of the products. The result is simple and delicious recipes accompanied by excellent wines. If you want to you can become really involved in life at the farm indulging in a spot of gardening and cheese making. Alternatively you can go fly fishing, explore the region on a Harley-Davidson or by horse-drawn carriage, not to mention the variety of beauty treatments available.

BLANTYRE

Located halfway between Boston and New York City this beautiful country house hotel is nestled amid 115 acres of lawn and woodlands.

Blantyre boasts a renowned cuisine and exceptional wine cellar and The Main House, Carriage House and four cottages are reminiscent of a gentler time of elegance and romance. This stately Tudor house was built in 1902 and is resplendent with luxurious guest rooms. The intimate, full treatment spa is connected to the Carriage House, a few minutes walk from the Tudor style Main House. This enchanting resort has activities galore, including tennis and croquet in the Summer. In the Winter, the property offers a Winter wonderland with ice skating, snowshoeing, sleigh riding and a Christmas tree 100 feet high.

BEDFORD POST INN

954 Old Post Road
Bedford, New York 10506
United States
Tel.:   + 1 914 205 3773
Fax: + 1 914 205 3775
E-mail: bedford@relais.com
Website: www.relais.com/bedford

BLACKBERRY FARM

1471 West Millers Cove
Walland, Tennessee 37886
United States
Tel.:   + 1 865 984 8166
Fax: + 1 865 681 7753
E-mail: blackberry@relais.com
Website: www.relais.com/blackberry

BLANTYRE

16 Blantyre Road, P.O. Box 995
Lenox, Massachusetts 01240
United States
Tel.:   + 1 413 637 3556
Fax: + 1 413 637 4282
E-mail: blantyre@relais.com
Website: www.relais.com/blantyre

THE SURREY HOTEL AND RESTAURANT

CANOE BAY

CASTLE HILL INN

Nestled in Manhattan's Upper East Side, The Surrey hotel is both a familiar destination and an unexpected delight. Built in 1926 as a residence hotel, the original Surrey was home to many of New York's most eccentric celebrities over the years. JFK. Bette Davis. Claudette Colbert. Famous faces who recognized the allure of exceptional, discreet service. Collaborating with acclaimed interior designer Lauren Rottet The Surrey paid special attention to maintaining the integrity of this history while modernizing what has become New York's most intimate address. Rottet's inspiration was a New York City townhouse passed down through the generations, the keeper of a lifetime of memories.

Inspired by chef Daniel Boulud's unique twist on time-honored French cuisine prepared with fine seasonal American ingredients, Café Boulud celebrates New York's café society with award-winning results. The restaurant's accolades include a star in the Michelin Guide and a 3-star review in The New York Times. The restaurant's menu reflects Boulud's four culinary muses: la tradition, classic French cuisine; la saison, seasonal delicacies; le potager, the vegetable garden; and le voyage, the flavors of world cuisines.

This hotel is a refuge for the most romantic souls.

Set on the banks of a wild and untouched lake, Canoe Bay plunges you into a preserved and enchanting part of Wisconsin where the simple pleasures – strolling through the woods, swimming in the lake, dining in the wine cellar, sampling great vintages – will shape your days. Forget cars and other modern means of transport ... here your vehicle is a canoe. This hotel offers a different rhythm, another way of looking at things, appreciating the time on your hands and feeling at one with nature. The lakeside terraces invite you to gaze at the view, daydream, or read, and the cedar interiors, flooded with light, soothe the senses.

You will always have a panoramic view of the deep blue of the Atlantic when you are at this magnificent resort, whether you are in your suite, relaxing on the terrace or sitting at a table in the restaurant.

Set in 16 hectares of grounds bordering the ocean, this hotel is a romantic haven of well-being. For a long time, this extraordinarily beautiful stretch of the ocean was the theater for America's Cup regattas. Local and regional cuisine plus exceptional wines are on the menu. Guests can also discover Newport, a magnet for music lovers from around the world, with its two festivals devoted to jazz and folk music.

THE SURREY HOTEL AND RESTAURANT
20 East 76th Street
New York, New York 10021
United States
Tel.: + 1 212 288 3700
Fax: + 1 646 358 3601
E-mail: surrey@relais.com
Website: www.relais.com/surrey

CANOE BAY
P.O. Box 28 Chetek
Wisconsin, 54728
United States
Tel.: + 1 715 924 4594
Fax: + 1 715 924 2078
E-mail: canoebay@relais.com
Website: www.relais.com/canoebay

CASTLE HILL INN
590 Ocean Drive
Newport, Rhode Island 02840
United States
Tel.: + 1 401 849 3800
Fax: + 1 401 849 3838
E-mail: castlehill@relais.com
Website: www.relais.com/castlehill

THE CHARLOTTE INN

CHATEAU DU SUREAU

CLIFTON

This is a captain's house in pure traditional British style in the heart of Martha's Vineyard, erstwhile haunt of whale hunters.

Ulysses Simpson Grant, Jackie Kennedy and Bill Clinton all fell under its charm. Offering a window into another time, which envelops you in its romantic atmosphere, the Charlotte Inn was built in 1864 for Samuel Osborne, a famous merchant. The staff, alert to the smallest detail, cultivate a deliciously old-fashioned elegance and courtesy. Antique lamps and exquisite silk or linen fabrics decorate the suites. Between one iced tea and the next on the flower-filled patio, go off to discover the wild island surrounding you, from its lighthouse to its beaches, ideal for waterskiing and kayaking.

You will love this majestic château, reminiscent of the finest châteaux in Europe.

It is ideally placed to explore the magnificent waterfalls and granite domes of Yosemite National Park – one of America's most spectacular natural sites. Château du Sureau's elegant interior, featuring guest rooms named after fragrant herbs and flowers, is resplendent with fine antiques, tapestries and artwork. Chef, Karsten Hart, showcases the freshest Californian produce in sophisticated, flavorful dishes, enhanced by a dash of the Mediterranean, and accompanied by the region's finest wines.

There is no doubt that you will fall under the spell of this part of the world when you stay in this lovely historic hotel built in 1799 – just like the three early presidents and founding fathers of the United States.

For it was in the Charlottesville Blue Ridge Mountains that Thomas Jefferson, James Madison and James Monroe built their homes. Clifton is set in 100 acres of woods, and the hotel prides itself on its understated elegance with its charming interior design and the warm beauty of its rooms and sites. Here, the murmur of the nearby Rivanna River, the gentle gurgle of the fountains and the soothing sounds of nature will surround you. On the program of this official trip: visiting historical residences (Monticello, Ashlawn-Highland and Montpelier) and renowned vineyards, a culinary cabaret at our Chef's Table, a game of croquet and refreshing dips in the infinity pool.

THE CHARLOTTE INN

27 South Summer Street, Box 1056
Edgartown, Massachusetts 02539
United States
Tel.:   + 1 508 627 4151
Fax: + 1 508 627 4652
E-mail: charlotte@relais.com
Website: www.relais.com/charlotte

CHÂTEAU DU SUREAU

48688 Victoria Lane
Oakhurst, Yosemite National Park
California 93644
United States
Tel.:   + 1 559 683 6860
Fax: + 1 559 683 0800
E-mail: sureau@relais.com
Website: www.relais.com/sureau

CLIFTON

1296 Clifton Inn Drive
Charlottesville, Virginia 22911
United States
Tel.:   + 1 434 971 1800
Fax: + 1 434 971 7098
E-mail: clifton@relais.com
Website: www.relais.com/clifton

COBBLERS COVE

DANIEL

DEL POSTO

Just a few steps away from a fine sandy beach edged by tropical gardens, Cobblers Cove on Barbados envelops you in English elegance with its marble floors, painted furniture, antique sofas and cushions embroidered with gold thread.

Here the days begin with a generous English breakfast and are then spent at your leisure with dips in the turquoise sea, water sports, beauty treatments and the pleasures of the table. At the poolside bar, tea time tends to be overshadowed by the delicious cocktails and excellent wines that just have to be tasted. There is also a special program of activities for children.

"Preparing the finest American ingredients according to French culinary tradition," is Daniel's mantra.

In Manhattan, Daniel Boulud's first name alone suffices for this Lyon native who is today one of America's most celebrated Chef-Restaurateurs. His reputation may be international, but his warm and welcoming style remains very personal. Chef Daniel Boulud magically combines humble and noble ingredients elevating rustic and heart warming dishes to new levels of refinement, sophistication and pleasure. This is home to French cuisine brought to life with a celebration of American regional ingredients like Montana beef, Oregon morels and Nantucket Bay scallops. Using his French technique, the unique flavors of these finest products become the spot light of Boulud's dishes.

Del Posto is the ultimate expression of what an Italian restaurant should be. Joe Bastianich, Lidia Bastianich and Mario Batali represent a convergence of different styles and experiences.
The restaurant concept generated at Del Posto can best be described as trans-generational: an expression of the evolution of cuisines, menus, service and ambiance that have characterized the history of the Italian dining experience in this country.

Del Posto creates the highest quality dining experience in what is one of the greatest indoor spaces in New York City. Without projecting stilted formality, Del Posto creates an ambiance filled with warmth, buoyancy and lightheartedness of the Italian spirit.

COBBLERS COVE

Road View
St. Peter (Caribbean) BB 26025
Barbados
Tel.:   + 1 246 422 2291
Fax: + 1 246 422 1460
E-mail: cobblers@relais.com
Website: www.relais.com/cobblers

DANIEL

60 East 65th Street
New York, New York 10065
United States
Tel.:   + 1 212 288 0033
Fax: + 1 212 396 9014
E-mail: danielnewyork@relais.com
Website: www.relais.com/danielnewyork

DEL POSTO

85 10th Avenue
New York, New York 10011
United States
Tel.:   + 1 212 497 8090
Fax: + 1 212 807 6320
E-mail: delposto@relais.com
Website: www.relais.com/delposto

EDEN ROCK - ST BARTHS

ELEVEN MADISON PARK

ESPERANZA RESORT

This is an ideal place for soaking up the sun of St Barths, lazing on the beach and exploring the dazzling undersea world.

Between the white sands and crystal clear waters of Saint-Jean Bay and located on a rocky promontory overlooking the coral reefs, this group of villas stands on the foundations of the former property of the aviator Rémy de Haenen, the first to land a plane on the island back in the 1940s. Jane and David Matthews have created the contemporary and eclectic interiors of the themed suites: the new Rockstar, with recording studio and the new Nina, the 'Fregate' with its private Jacuzzi, the Howard Hughes ...

Executive Chef Daniel Humm's philosophy is to sublimely enhance seasonal products.

What else? A simply remarkable wine list! A blend of colors, a melting pot of civilizations, cosmopolitan influences: it's here, in the very heart of Manhattan.
In a spectacular art deco building overlooking Madison Square Park, Executive Chef Daniel Humm draws his culinary inspiration and purely expresses 'the spirit of grand New York'. As master of ceremonies at Eleven Madison Park, Daniel Humm creates modern, sophisticated French cuisine, revisiting classical flavors with a magical pinch of 'je ne sais quoi'.

At the tip of Baja peninsula, in the heart of 17 hectares of unspoilt nature in the private enclave of Punta Ballena, lies Esperanza, which is located 4 miles from Cabo San Lucas.

All its 57 casitas and suites are tucked away on small hills and boast exceptional views of the ocean, into which the infinity pool seems to simply disappear. With so many alternatives at your beck and call, whether it be enjoying the private beach, the spa, the art gallery or the golf courses, you will simply have no time for boredom. In the evening, unwind and admire the sunset while sipping a delicious cocktail before savoring gourmet cuisine in the idyllic setting of the restaurant.

EDEN ROCK - ST BARTHS

St Jean
Saint-Barthélemy 97133
French West Indies
Tel.: + 590 (0)5 90 29 79 99
Fax: + 590 (0)5 90 27 88 37
E-mail: edenrock@relais.com
Website: www.relais.com/edenrock

ELEVEN MADISON PARK

11 Madison Avenue
New York, New York 10010
United States
Tel.: + 1 212 889 2535
Fax: + 1 212 889 0918
E-mail: eleven@relais.com
Website: www.relais.com/eleven

ESPERANZA RESORT

Carretera Transpeninsular Km 7 Manzana
Punta Ballena, Cabo San Lucas
Baja, California 23410
Mexico
Tel.: + 52 62414 56400
Fax: + 52 62414 56499
E-mail: esperanza@relais.com
Website: www.relais.com/esperanza

EVEREST

This stylishly decorated restaurant offers breathtaking views and flavors. Chief/proprietor Jean Joho embodies the American dream.

This Frenchman from Alsace is now one of the most respected chefs on the continent after coming to the United States almost 25 years ago. Like a symbol of his success and the giddy heights that his cuisine has reached, Everest is situated on the 40th floor of the Chicago Stock Exchange. Jean Joho endlessly reinvents the great classics of French cuisine. His hallmark is to combine noble products like foie gras or caviar with the humble potato and turnip to create delicious surprises. In honour of his homeland, wines from Alsace also star in many of his recipes such as his Wasserstriwela smoked Arctic Char on a bed of paprika-infused sauerkraut or Casco Bay Sea Scallops with Belgian chicory, Melfor and Gewurztraminer.

THE FRENCH LAUNDRY

With the herbs and vegetables straight from the garden, don't be surprised by the freshness that bursts in your mouth.

At the heart of Napa Valley, Thomas Keller, who also welcomes guests in New York with his Per Se restaurant, has established one of the best tables in California. Thomas Keller's technique has become so famous that Pixar studios called upon his expertise when making the film Ratatouille. You may not get a chance to taste it in his restaurant The French Laundry, but the revisited ratatouille served at the end of the film is his invention. Working closely with Chef de Cuisine, Timothy Hollingsworth, and the best producers in the region, he and his team concoct voluntarily minimalist dishes, where products such as oysters and truffles are savored in a series of scripted mouthfuls. The idea behind this 'sequencing' of the meal is to multiply the surprises in a restaurant that renews its menu every day.

GARY DANKO

Described as the ambassador of contemporary American fine dining, the cuisine of Gary Danko draws on culinary traditions from around the world.

Roast quail stuffed with morels, leeks and pine nuts, steamed shellfish with a Thai curry, seared sea scallops with Spring vegetables. Using seasonings from Asia and India, he adds a pinch of audacity to his French-style precision and technique. The results are sublime and balanced, often showcasing strictly seasonal flavors such as his foie gras served with cherries in Spring and roast figs in Fall. The food is pure sophistication, to be savored in an intimate and welcoming ambience – taupe walls enhanced by modern paintings – in one of San Francisco's trendiest districts.

EVEREST
440 South LaSalle Street
Chicago, Illinois 60605
United States
Tel.:   + 1 312 663 8920
Fax: + 1 312 663 8802
E-mail: everest@relais.com
Website: www.relais.com/everest

THE FRENCH LAUNDRY
6640 Washington Street
Yountville, California 94599
United States
Tel.:   + 1 707 944 2380
Fax: + 1 707 944 1974
E-mail: laundry@relais.com
Website: www.relais.com/laundry

GARY DANKO
800 North Point
San Francisco, California 94109
United States
Tel.:   + 1 415 749 2060
Fax: + 1 415 775 1805
E-mail: danko@relais.com
Website: www.relais.com/danko

GLENDORN

Built in the 1920s, this inn has kept all its original charm and authenticity and is situated in a gorgeously green and unspoilt part of Pennsylvania, halfway between Pittsburgh and Buffalo.

On the program are walks in the fresh air, fly fishing at Lake Bondieu (just a few minutes away), Pennsylvanian clay pigeon shooting, snooker ... and total rest. The main lodge and individual chalets are built with sequoia wood and blend perfectly into the breathtaking natural surroundings: a forest of hemlock spruces where it is not rare to spot foxes, deer or beavers, and you will be lulled by the soothing murmur of bubbling streams.

GLENMERE MANSION

In the heart of farmland, perched on a Catskill Mountain sits this 150-acre estate where past meets present in grandiose fashion.

Just an hour away from New York City, this sumptuous hotel and spa – one of America's finest country homes, once host to royalty, aristocracy, and leading artists. Now reborn as a premier luxury hotel the renovated property boasts the finest linens, furniture, porcelain and private modern art collection. Renowned chefs offer a wealth of dishes straight from 'farm to table' in two restaurants. Magnificent formal gardens, spectacular pool, tennis, bocce, croquet courts make this the ultimate romantic Hudson Valley getaway.

HASTINGS HOUSE COUNTRY HOUSE HOTEL

Hastings House Country House Hotel is situated on picturesque Salt Spring Island just off Vancouver Island. The charming waterfront resort lies on nearly nine hectares of lovingly tended gardens, forest and pasture overlooking Ganges Harbour. A magnificent 11th Century Sussex-style manor house built by British architect Warren Hastings in 1940, is the heart of the property and a convivial spot for cocktails and dining.

Its quaint inglenook fireplace and other authentic British details are embellished with original antiques and the work of local artists. The resort has 18 suites and rooms located in the main house or nearby historic outbuildings. Hastings House makes a sensational base for exploring British Columbia's landscape, while the island itself is a hotspot for artists and locavores. The hotel's restaurant serves outstanding regional fare courtesy of executive chef Marcel Kauer, featuring fresh produce picked from its own gardens.

GLENDORN
1000 Glendorn Drive
Bradford, Pennsylvania 16701
United States
Tel.:   + 1 814 362 6511
Fax: + 1 814 368 9923
E-mail: glendorn@relais.com
Website: www.relais.com/glendorn

GLENMERE MANSION
P.O. Box 170, 634 Pine Hill Road
Chester, New York 10918
United States
Tel.:   + 1 845 469 1900
Fax: + 1 845 469 1919
E-mail: glenmere@relais.com
Website: www.relais.com/glenmere

HASTINGS HOUSE COUNTRY HOUSE HOTEL
160 Upper Ganges Road
Salt Spring Island, British Columbia V8K 2S2
Canada
Tel.:   + 1 250 537 2362
Fax: + 1 250 537 533
E-mail: hastings@relais.com
Website: www.relais.com/hastingshouse

HOMESTEAD INN

HORNED DORSET PRIMAVERA

HOTEL FAUCHERE

The Homestead Inn is a beautiful 18th century Victorian manor house situated near the waters of Long Island and Thomas Henkelmann is the most French of German chefs.

Born in the Black Forest, this devotee of French gastronomy learned his trade in Alsace before moving his pots and pans to Connecticut. Inspired by his travels, each of his recipes makes a veiled reference to his origins. Thomas Henkelmann likes to break down boundaries between products and to create surprising combinations, such as his champagne sauerkraut accompanied by a seafood mousseline. His partner Theresa – an interior designer – has turned this hotel into a setting worthy of his cooking by creating a European atmosphere inspired by Balinese and Chinese styles. This must be Greenwich's most tasteful address.

Lovely beaches, where swimming is superb, nearby casinos and golf (on Eisenhower's favorite course complete the experience at The Horned Dorset Primavera.

With its elegant and classic neo-colonial architecture this hotel looks out at the Straits of Mona, in a part of the island where, nearby, the curling waves are a surfer's dream. Your duplex suite offers a contrast between the dark glossy woods and the pure white veils that envelop your four poster bed. Your suite includes a terrace with private swimming pool and two bathrooms. The hotel is spread out on hilly terrain with charming places to relax such as the library, the veranda, the bar with its terrace next to the sea and the gourmet restaurant.

The Hotel Fauchère is a casually elegant destination with exquisite cuisine offering two restaurants, a pâtisserie, 16 superbly-restored guest rooms (marble baths, heated towel racks, Kiehl's amenities, Frette linens) and adjacent meeting facilities.

Founded in 1852 by Delmonico's Master Chef, Louis Fauchère, and run by his descendants until closing in 1976, the hotel's extraordinary culinary legacy was reclaimed in 2006 after a meticulous five-year restoration. The Delmonico Room offers a contemporary interpretation of the classics, while the sleek, minimalist Bar Louis – with a giant photograph of Andy Warhol and John Lennon above the bar – features bistro-style global cuisine, including Sushi Pizza, its signature dish. Within walking and hiking distance are historic attractions, shopping, important architecture and the north gate to a 70,000 acre national park with its spectacular waterfalls.

THOMAS HENKELMANN – HOMESTEAD INN
420 Field Point Road
Greenwich, Connecticut 06830
United States
Tel.:   + 1 203 869 7500
Fax: + 1 203 869 7502
E-mail: homestead@relais.com
Website: www.relais.com/homestead

HORNED DORSET PRIMAVERA
Route 429, km 30
Rincon 00677
Puerto Rico
Tel.:   + 1 787 823 40 30
Fax: + 1 787 823 55 80
E-mail: horneddorset@relais.com
Website: www.relais.com/horneddorset

HOTEL FAUCHERE
401 Broad Street
Milford, Pennsylvania 18337
United States
Tel.:   + 1 570 409 1212
Fax: + 1 570 409 1251
E-mail: fauchere@relais.com
Website: www.relais.com/fauchere

HOTEL LE TOINY

HOTEL ST GERMAIN

THE INN OF THE FIVE GRACES

This is a true paradise nestled into the hills of 'Saint Barth', in the heart of a 17 hectare estate and its palm grove.

"True idleness means getting up at 6am so you have more time to do nothing," wrote Tristan Bernard. This is the frame of mind you can adopt at the Hôtel Le Toiny. Your refuge: one of the 15 colonial-style villa suites overlooking the sea. In the infinity pool or on the white sandy beach, bathing is a moment of sheer bliss before treating yourself to a massage on your private terrace. The same splendor is carried over into the meals in the gourmet restaurant Le Gaïac where Chef Stéphane Mazières skillfully enhances the flavors.

Recently classified as a historical landmark, Hôtel St Germain was built in 1906 as a private residence for a prominent local family.

Truly a cosmopolitan retreat, Hotel St Germain is merely steps away from the bustle of the Dallas Center for the Performing Arts, the Winspear Opera House and Meyerson Symphony Center. It has the sumptuous allure of a French hotel with exceptional old world service, thoroughly modern amenities and memorable fine dining. The gracefully appointed interiors combine to evoke the haunting, exotic beauty of 19th century New Orleans. Hôtel St Germain is a true European urban sanctuary, which offers a unique destination experience, where fine dining and the art of gracious living are celebrated and are a personal reflection of the proprietors' French heritage.

Located in the historic district of Santa Fe, The Inn of the Five Graces combines luxury with an aura of mystery.

With an ethnic decor enhanced by East Indian and Tibetan antiques, oriental carpets and nomadic textiles combined with Southwest architecture, the interiors feature many handcrafted pieces as well as spectacular tile mosaics. Santa Fe is the second oldest town in the U.S. and is still very much influenced by its Indian and Spanish heritage. It possesses that true 'Pueblo' charm, with its narrow streets, patios and typical ochre-colored houses. It is above all a town of art and culture where you can also enjoy a private concert at the opera house or discover the works of numerous painters and sculptors. Passionate about this land with its wealth of Indian legends, the owners invite you to embark on a sensory voyage to fully savor this melting pot of cultures and colors. One of the possibilities: take lessons with a professional photographer and capture the incredible beauty of the landscapes.

HOTEL LE TOINY

Anse de Toiny
Saint-Barthélemy 97133
French West Indies
Tel.:   + 590 5 90 27 88 88
Fax: + 590 5 90 27 89 30
E-mail: toiny@relais.com
Website: www.relais.com/toiny

HOTEL ST GERMAIN

2516 Maple Avenue
Dallas, Texas 75201
United States
Tel.:   + 1 214 871 2516
Fax: + 1 214 871 0740
E-mail: saint-germain@relais.com
Website: www.relais.com/saint-germain

THE INN OF THE FIVE GRACES

150 East De Vargas Street
Santa Fe, New Mexico 87501
United States
Tel.:   + 1 505 992 0957
Fax: + 1 505 955 0549
E-mail: fivegraces@relais.com
Website: www.relais.com/fivegraces

JEAN GEORGES

KINGSBRAE ARMS

L'AUBERGE CARMEL

The Jean Georges restaurant has become an absolute must in Manhattan. 'Genius' for some and 'great master of gastronomy' for others, Jean-Georges Vongerichten is a chef who generates superlatives.

The interior design is Zen, revealing the artist's love of streamlined elegance and Asia. Indeed this Frenchman is famous for his 'Thai-French cuisine'. A fusion of two great culinary traditions that produces breathtaking results: red and white tuna marinated in olive oil and lemon juice, foie gras brûlée in a cherry sauce with a white port jelly, black bass and radish bulb salad, candied fruits accompanied by homemade orange zest and kiwi sorbets ... It is impossible to tell you anything more about the menu: Jean-Georges reinvents it every three months.

New Brunswick is one of the most beautiful parts of Canada, famous for its tides that reach record heights – 14 metres in some places – its constantly changing beaches and its coast inhabited by whales.

Kingsbrae is a private and romantic country house built in 1897 on the heights of St. Andrews, overlooking the little harbor below. It is decorated in polished wood and marble and features period fireplaces, four-poster beds and precious objects. Between dinners that celebrate the sea and Chef's organic garden and massages with essential oils, discover the famous botanical garden of Kingsbrae containing, within 11 hectares, almost 50,000 species of flowers, a series of footpaths, a Dutch windmill, a maze of cedar trees and various other horticultural treasures.

It was in front of the stunning scenery of Big Sur that Henry Miller said that he learnt to pray. Drop your bags at a romantic hotel, L'Auberge Carmel, which was built in 1929.

In the little village of artists of Carmel-by-the-Sea it is the ideal base to take the time to meditate in front of the immensity of the cliffs which seem to plunge down into the ocean. Halfway between San Francisco and the coast of Santa Barbara, inhabited by seals, whales and other marine mammals, the village – where Clint Eastwood was once mayor – will charm you with its many art galleries and pebble beaches. The interior designer Kathleen Fink has decorated it with the most beautiful antiques and fabrics from Europe. Delicious cuisine, a wine cellar with over 4,500 bottles, massages and a short stroll to Carmel beach will give this address a special place in your heart, in the footsteps of the author.

JEAN GEORGES
One Central Park West
New York, New York 10023
United States
Tel.: + 1 212 299 3900
Fax: + 1 212 299 3914
E-mail: jeangeorges@relais.com
Website: www.relais.com/jeangeorges

KINGSBRAE ARMS
219 King Street, St Andrews
New Brunswick E5B 1Y1
Canada
Tel.: + 1 506 529 1897
Fax: + 1 506 529 1197
E-mail: kingsbrae@relais.com
Website: www.relais.com/kingsbrae

L'AUBERGE CARMEL
Monte Verde Street, at 7th Avenue Carmel
California 93921
United States
Tel.: + 1 831 624 8578
Fax: + 1 831 626 1018
E-mail: carmel@relais.com
Website: www.relais.com/carmel

LAKE PLACID LODGE

LANGDON HALL COUNTRY HOUSE HOTEL & SPA

LAS MANANITAS HOTEL GARDEN RESTAURANT & SPA

Situated on the shores of Lake Placid, The Lake Placid Lodge is a beautifully handcrafted Lodge nestled in the Adirondack Mountains.

A remarkable arts and crafts style lodge, the Main Lodge offers the finest accommodation and dining in a comfortably rustic, yet refined setting. Pamper yourself in the Main Lodge, the private cabins or the remodelled Lakeside suites, offering gorgeous views of Lake Placid and Whiteface Mountain. The guest rooms, suites and cabins feature luxurious featherbeds, wood burning fireplaces, rustic furnishings, and deep soaking baths. The Dining Room offers a prix-fixe menu with dining available on the deck overlooking Lake Placid and Whiteface Mountain. For a relaxed setting try the 'Pub' which serves lunch, dinner and an all day menu, and also offers outside dining on the deck.

Just an hour and a half drive from Toronto and the Niagara area, this is the address for those who love beauty. Epicurean and romantic are the best words to describe Langdon Hall.

Romantic with its gracious interiors of warm tones, silky fabrics and wood panelling detail, its tranquil grounds and gardens, where one can sit under a century old elm tree sipping fine wine or relax by the lily pond reflecting the elegant lines of the manor. And epicurean with its exceptional cuisine. In the kitchen, every detail counts for young Chef Jonathan Gushue, who even makes his own butter and, as a result, each meal is an unforgettable moment. As a devotee of French cuisine, his favourite ingredients include truffles, foie gras, frogs' legs, snails and artisanal cheeses all of which he turns into sophisticated compositions that match the elegance of the setting. For added relaxation, the spa offers the very best in body and beauty therapies.

Right in the center of Cuernavaca, nicknamed the "city of eternal Spring" because of the mildness of its climate, is a sumptuous hacienda in the purest Mexican tradition.

In the exotic gardens, among the sculptures by Francisco Zuñiga and lush flowers, you can admire peacocks strutting about near the fountains and blue parrots perched in the trees. Under their tiled roofs, the villas and their colonial suites are decorated with some of the country's most beautiful antiques and artworks including paintings by José Luis Cuevas, Leonardo Nierman and Carlos Mérida. Your itinerary: a typical and abundant cuisine and a choice of excursions on the trail of the Aztecs, including a visit to the Palace of Cortès and exploration of the ruined cities of Xochicalco and Taxco - famous for its silversmiths and silver shops.

LAKE PLACID LODGE

Whiteface Inn Road, P.O. Box 550
Lake Placid, New York 12946
United States
Tel.: + 1 518 523 2700
Fax: + 1 518 523 1124
E-mail: lakeplacid@relais.com
Website: www.relais.com/lakeplacid

LANGDON HALL COUNTRY HOUSE
HOTEL & SPA

RR n°33 Cambridge
Ontario N3H 4R8
Canada
Tel.: + 1 519 740 2100
Fax: + 1 519 740 8161
E-mail: langdon@relais.com
Website: www.relais.com/langdon

LAS MANANITAS HOTEL
GARDEN RESTAURANT & SPA

Ricardo Linares 107 Col.
Centro, Cuernavaca, Morelos 62000
Mexico
Tel.: + 52 777 362 00 00
Fax: + 52 777 318 36 72
E-mail: mananitas@relais.com
Website: www.relais.com/mananitas

MANOIR HOVEY

This is a wonderful getaway in all seasons only 80 minutes from Montreal.

Manoir Hovey, a historic mansion, is nestled among English gardens and forest on 600 meters of lakeshore and inspires a romantic and relaxing lifestyle reminiscent of its origins as a private estate (with all the modern luxuries added). Rates include an abundance of year-round recreational facilities on site making the Manoir a destination in itself. The culinary arts are scrupulously upheld, enhanced by an 850 reference wine list and an exceptional selection of Québec cheeses. A stay at Manoir Hovey comes with the promise of an abundance of fresh air in a scenic, unspoilt part of Québec very near to Montreal and the U.S.-Canadian border.

MAREA

Situated on the south side of New York's Central Park, Marea attracts gourmets from around the world thanks to it exquisite Italian-inspired seafood, served in an elegant but relaxed setting.

Grand chef Michael White is the culinary force behind Marea, which as its name – 'tide' in Italian indicates; it is a tribute to the sea. The menu starts off with a mouth-watering selection of crudo (raw fish), and continues with delectable pasta dishes such as spaghetti with crab and Santa Barbara sea urchin and then offers a selection of main fish courses as well as whole fish. Part of the joy of Marea is its stunning ambience. Crisp white table clothes meet warm lighting and design features including a dramatic bar made from Egyptian onyx, wall panelling fashioned out of lacquered Indonesian rosewood and hand-dipped silver seashells as window ornaments.

MEADOWOOD NAPA VALLEY

The Napa Valley is one of the most prestigious wine-producing areas in the United States due to its Mediterranean climate and extremely fertile soil.

It has a viticultural heritage dating back to the 19th century. At Meadowood, you will find yourself at the heart of a unique tasting journey, starting with the estate's very own wine educator, who loves to share his passion. And for culinary delights 'The Restaurant at Meadowood' is one of the best in the region. The cosy lodges, guestrooms or suites with patios and views of the trees or the fairways – everything comes together to ensure sweet dreams among Redwoods, California 'LiveOak' trees, Big Leaf Maple trees and Douglas Fir.

MANOIR HOVEY
575 Hovey Road
North Hatley, Québec J0B 2C0
Canada
Tel.:   + 1 819 842 2421
Fax: + 1 819 842 2248
E-mail: hovey@relais.com
Website: www.relais.com/hovey

MAREA
240 Central Park South
New York, NY 10019
United States
Tel.:   + 1 212.582.5100
Fax: + 1 212.582.5177
E-mail: marea@relais.com
Website: www.relais.com/marea

MEADOWOOD NAPA VALLEY
900 Meadowood Lane
St. Helena, California 94574
United States
Tel.:   + 1 707 963 3646
Fax: + 1 707 963 3532
E-mail: meadowood@relais.com
Website: www.relais.com/meadowood

MENTON

A blend of French discipline and Italian passion reflect the restaurant's namesake, a French seaside town near the Italian border. Located in Fort Point, the neighborhood's urban cityscape, with its blend of historic brick buildings and sleek, futuristic design statements, is the perfect setting for Menton, a modern interpretation of fine dining. With beautifully executed cuisine, an unparalleled wine program, gracious hospitality and a glamorous setting, Menton seeks to excite, inspire, and transport guests for one memorable evening.

Just as the chefs carefully source each ingredient, every element of the space, from the French linens to the Austrian wine glasses, has also been thoughtfully selected to enhance the entire dining experience. In addition to the Dining Room, Menton offers the Chef's Table, which provides a brilliant vantage point from which to observe the kitchen, and the Private Dining Room, for memorable private events.

MONTPELIER PLANTATION

This former sugar plantation where Admiral Nelson married Fanny Nisbet in 1787 is located at the foot of Nevis Peak – a volcano that has fallen into a deep sleep.

Today, the lush vegetation has reclaimed the slopes and this magnificently restored residence is a haven of romanticism. Stay in a delightfully elegant cottage and savor international Caribbean cuisine on the terrace or in the old mill overlooking the pool. When you are not swimming on the private beach, you are sure to enjoy strolling around the tropical gardens or walking, hand in hand, around the ruins of the old plantation.

OCEAN HOUSE

The Ocean House sits high on the bluffs of Watch Hill, Rhode Island, overlooking a private stretch of beach with sweeping views of the Atlantic Ocean, Montauk and Block Island.

Inspired by the Victorian architecture prevalent in the great houses of the Watch Hill area, the Ocean House evokes a timeless elegance that captures the residential ambiance of the area's turn of the century summer estates. Beautifully appointed and casually elegant Ocean House brings together British Colonial style, early American and seaside aesthetics in sundrenched colors of yellow, blue, turquoise and cream. Public spaces are adorned with a stunning, rotating, multi-million dollar art collection. The exterior, designed in the classic Victorian style of the original hotel, couples red-cedar shingled roofs with wide verandahs and features historically accurate reproduction accents to complement the rich history of Watch Hill.

MENTON

354, Congress Street
Boston, Massachusetts 02210
United States
Tel.:   + 1 617 737 0099
Fax: + 1 617 737 0089
E-mail: menton@relais.com
Website: www.relais.com/menton

MONTPELIER PLANTATION

P.O. Box 474
Charlestown, Nevis
St Kitts & Nevis
Tel.:   + 1 869 469 3462
Fax: + 1 869 469 2932
E-mail: montpelier@relais.com
Website: www.relais.com/montpelier

OCEAN HOUSE

1 Bluff Avenue
Watch Hill, Rhode Island 02891
United States
Tel.:   + 1 401 584 7000
Fax: + 1 401 584 7044
E-mail: oceanhouse@relais.com
Website: www.relais.com/oceanhouse

PATINA	PER SE	POST HOTEL & SPA

Californian cuisine is infused with European influences in this elegant restaurant with its pure and modern decor.

Inside the huge Walt Disney Concert Hall – a steel complex of venues at the heart of Los Angeles – the renowned German Chef Joachim Splichal has created one of the city's most prized tables. The trademark of Patina is fresh seasonal products highlighted by sophisticated presentations. The flavors are distinct in each dish, sweet or salty, but are always magnified by herbs, exotic spices or bursts of acidity such as in the grilled Scottish salmon with baby artichokes and blood orange, or the Mediterranean loup de mer with minestrone and pesto croutons. The caviar guéridon and the variety of cheeses are two other reasons to visit this prestigious address.

Per Se offers a festival of culinary delights that will convince you perfection does indeed exist.

Following the success of his California restaurant, The French Laundry, Thomas Keller brought his distinctive hands-on approach from the Napa Valley to New York City, reflecting an intense focus on detail, extending not only to cuisine, but also to presentation, mood and surroundings. Chef de Cuisine Eli Kaimeh interprets modern American recipes with a touch of French influence in the elegant dining room with a view of Central Park. Representative dishes include 'Oysters and Pearls', a sabayon of pearl tapioca with poached oysters and caviar and 'Calotte de Boeuf Grillée' with crispy bone marrow, russet potato mille-feuille and forest mushrooms with sauce bordelaise ... "A good meal is not only about good food and good wine. Above it all should be an emotional experience," asserts Thomas Keller.

Offering a stunning panorama of the Canadian Rockies, the Post Hotel is nestled in a beautiful valley in Banff National Park.

Just a few kilometers from famous Lake Louise with its magnificent palette of emerald greens, the hotel's little log cabins with their red roofs overlook the Pipestone River. This is a mountain lodge at its finest where the comfy and romantic interiors make way for spacious suites in pale wood, always stocked with a good supply of logs to warm up your evenings. If your muscles are complaining after a few long ski runs, ice skating on the lake or snowshoeing to spot the nearby elk, deer or moose, a visit to the Hotel's Temple Mountain Spa will surely soothe. For the more adventurous, helicopter skiing is not far away. Enjoy the award-winning menu based on fresh produce and local game.

PATINA
141 South Grand Avenue
Los Angeles, California 90012
United States
Tel.:   + 1 213 972 3331
Fax: + 1 213 972 3531
E-mail: patina@relais.com
Website: www.relais.com/patina

PER SE
10 Columbus Circle
4th floor, New York 10019
United States
Tel.:   + 1 212 823 9335
Fax: + 1 212 823 9353
E-mail: perse@relais.com
Website: www.relais.com/perse

POST HOTEL & SPA
P.O. Box 69
Lake Louise, Alberta TOL 1EO
Canada
Tel.:   + 1 403 522 3989
Fax: + 1 403 522 3966
E-mail: posthotel@relais.com
Website: www.relais.com/posthotel

QUINCE RESTAURANT

Owned by husband-and-wife team Michael and Lindsay Tusk, Quince is an award winning restaurant situated in an historic 1907 brick and timber building located in the storied Jackson Square neighborhood of San Francisco, California.

An elegant, sophisticated space, Quince's historical architectural elements of arched brick walls and soaring ceilings provide contrast with warm, grey and chocolate hues, luxurious Christian Liaigre chairs and velveteen banquettes, dramatic Venetian chandeliers and large-format art work by notable artists. The Quince photography collection includes works from Candida Hoeffer, Vic Munioz, Sally Mann, Lee Friedlander and Joanne Veerburg.

The striking architecture of the building, together with its modern interiors, provide a stunning venue to enjoy Michael Tusk's daily changing Italian and French-inspired menu that celebrates the seasonal bounty of Northern California.

RANCHO VALENCIA

This traditional farm is deep in Tennessee and offers a chance to return to nature and rediscover life's simple pleasures. Guests are treated to a steady flow of deliciously fresh produce all year round as part of the 1700 hectares of land set aside for farming.

In addition to vegetables, cheese, herbs, honey, cider and much more are all produced right here. Established ties with local gardeners and tradespeople mean that Blackberry Farm's team of Chefs offers a menu that respects the authenticity of the flavors and the integrity of the products. The result is simple and delicious recipes accompanied by excellent wines. If you want to you can become really involved in life at the farm indulging in a spot of gardening and cheese making. Alternatively you can go fly fishing, explore the region on a Harley-Davidson or by horse-drawn carriage, not to mention the variety of beauty treatments available.

RESTAURANT EUROPEA

Restaurant Europea celebrates ten years of extraordinary cuisine.

Experience the art of hospitality and enjoy a creative French gourmet cuisine inspired by local ingredients. Chosen as one of the World top 10 restaurants by the 2012 Travelers' Choice Awards on Trip advisor web site, Europea remains one of the best dining choices in Montreal. The contemporary and elegant restaurant, situated in a beautiful Victorian house in the heart of downtown Montreal, also joined the ranks of the distinguished Relais & Châteaux family just over a year ago. Celebrated chef Jérôme Ferrer continues to charm his clients with his love of entertaining and his inventive gourmet cuisine using local ingredients.

QUINCE RESTAURANT

470 Pacific Avenue
San Francisco, California 94133
United States
Tel.: + 1 415.775.8500
Fax: + 1 415.775.8501
E-mail: quince@relais.com
Website: www.relais.com/quince

RANCHO VALENCIA

5921 Valencia Circle, P.O. Box 9126
Rancho, Santa Fe, California 92067
United States
Tel.: + 1 858 756 1123
Fax: + 1 858 756 0165
E-mail: valencia@relais.com
Website: www.relais.com/valencia

RESTAURANT EUROPEA

1227 De la Montagne
Montréal, Québec H3G 1Z2
Canada
Tel.: + 1 514 398 9229
Fax: + 1 514 398 9718
E-mail: europea@relais.com
Website: www.relais.com/europea

RESTAURANT INITIALE INC.

RESTAURANT TOQUE!

SONORA RESORT CANADA

Originally from the little fishing village of Cancale in Brittany, Yvan Lebrun and his partner Rolande, have created one of the best restaurants in North America.

Yvan Lebrun's motto is 'simplicity and precision'. His love of food and the pure delight of his guests spurs him on to combine the very best of French and Québec culinary tradition. Here, hearts of palm are made into flour, dandelion honey becomes a smooth ice cream, maple syrup appears regularly in harmonious creations and, of course, oysters have a starring role.

With its light-filled dining room and its contemporary atmosphere, the restaurant Toqué is the meeting place for gourmets in search of new flavors to share with friends right in the heart of Montréal.

The Chef, Normand Laprise, is far from being a solitary artist. He supports local suppliers and farmers through his cuisine, true artisans of taste who help turn his culinary experiences into truly great moments of discovery. Vegetables, wild herbs, seafood, wild mushrooms, edible flowers, duck, beef, lamb, fish... The finest products from Québec are featured with photos of the various dishes displayed on the menu. Accompanied by a superb, audacious wine list. The taste of Québec in all its freshness!

A jewel of the very purest caliber Sonora Resort is nestled in the heart of an archipelago between Vancouver Island and the west coast of Canada.

Accessible only by sea and air the enchantment already begins during the transfer to the hotel with no roads or villas on the horizon. The guest rooms offer breathtaking views at any time of the day of unspoilt, wild nature. Watch eagles, seals, bears, the green emerald of the sea and forests, the limpid streams, snowy mountain tops that seem to cast themselves straight into the sea. The wild landscapes, combined with the indoor luxury, are the elements that make up the magical alchemy of this unique region. The comfort and the elegance of the lodges are carried through to the smallest detail of the colors and materials. An absolute paradise for angling enthusiasts, Sonora Resort offers a wide range of sporting and leisure activities. How delightful it is to intersperse days spent in the fresh, outdoor air with pampering visits to the unique, upscale spa dedicated to wellness or by taking a dip in the outdoor heated pool.

RESTAURANT INITIALE INC.

54 rue Saint-Pierre
Québec, G1K 4A1
Canada
Tel.:   + 1 418 694 1818
Fax: + 1 418 694 2387
E-mail: initiale@relais.com
Website: www.relais.com/initiale

RESTAURANT TOQUE!

900 place Jean-Paul-Riopelle
Montréal, Québec H2Z 2B2
Canada
Tel.:   + 1 514 499 2084
Fax: + 1 514 499 0292
E-mail: toque@relais.com
Website: www.relais.com/toque

SONORA RESORT CANADA

4580 Cowley Crescent
Richmond, British Columbia V7B 1B8
Canada
Tel.:   + 1 604 233 0460
Fax: + 1 604 233 0465
E-mail: sonora@relais.com
Website: www.relais.com/sonora

THE FEARRINGTON HOUSE INN, RESTAURANT & SPA

THE HOME RANCH

THE INN AT LITTLE WASHINGTON

This is a made-to-measure retreat for lovers of good food, fine wine and gracious hospitality.

The farm-like setting with white facades, rocking chairs, lush landscaping and intimate courtyards will transport you to a place far away from the ordinary. Inspired by their travels abroad, R.B. Fitch and his late wife transformed a central North Carolina farm into a charming, elegant village, replete with shops, restaurants and the award-winning Fearrington House Inn and Restaurant. It is situated near one of the country's most dynamic research and venture capital hubs – the Research Triangle region encompassing Raleigh and Durham. You can discover the Jordan Lake nature preserve and nearby Chapel Hill, home to the nation's oldest state university among author readings, spa treatments, shopping and customized wine dinners.

Admire stunning views of the Rockies from your cosy room and the magnificent hand-hewn log lodge – mountains made famous by so many great Westerns.

As you gallop horseback across the splendid terrain, transport yourself to another world: you are the cowboy. Back at the ranch, dive into the pool or try your hand at fly-fishing, and enjoy a remarkable breakfast, lunch and dinner prepared under the direction of the chef.

Just an hour's drive from Washington, D.C., this sumptuous hotel nestled at the foot of the Blue Ridge Mountains is a great retreat with its princely suites and opulent lounges hung with 18th century paintings and tapestries.

"When I was younger, I wanted to be an actor," remembers chef and owner Patrick O'Connell. But a love of cooking would send this dream off course. But no regrets: "A restaurant is a real living theater, where I can play out various roles." Patrick is actor, director and producer of the show which runs every day in his dining room. His scripted menus put the spotlight on his Refined American Cuisine, such as Medallions of Rabbit Loin Wrapped in House Cured Pancetta Surrounding a Lilliputian Rabbit Rib Roast Resting on a Pillow of Pea Purée.

THE FEARRINGTON HOUSE INN, RESTAURANT & SPA

2000 Fearrington Village
Pittsboro, North Carolina 27312
United States
Tel.:   + 1 919 542 2121
Fax: + 1 919 542 4202
E-mail: fearrington@relais.com
Website: www.relais.com/fearrington

THE HOME RANCH

P.O. Box 822
Clark, Colorado 80428
United States
Tel.:   + 1 970 879 1780
Fax: + 1 970 879 1795
E-mail: homeranch@relais.com
Website: www.relais.com/homeranch

THE INN AT LITTLE WASHINGTON

Middle and Main Streets, P.O. Box 300
Washington, Virginia 22747
United States
Tel.:   + 1 540 675 3800
Fax: + 1 540 675 3100
E-mail: washington@relais.com
Website: www.relais.com/washington

THE MAYFLOWER INN & SPA

THE PITCHER INN

PLANTERS INN

This property is one of the most acclaimed destination spas in the U.S. and is nestled on 58 acres of lush grounds less than two hours from the Big Apple.

Enjoy an amazing array of treatments as well as classes in dream interpretation, dance, painting, writing, yoga and Tai Chi among others in the spa with its stunning decor, enhanced by a calming palette of blue and white. Workshops on topics such as marriage, sleep and stress are led by renowned experts in their respective fields. The culinary offering includes the healthy and delicious cuisine of the spa as well as the fine dining experience available at The Inn, and the guest rooms reflect the tranquil elegance evident throughout the property.

Set among Vermont's Green Mountains, The Pitcher Inn is a delightfully distinctive and elegant hotel that celebrates intellectual curiosity, culinary excellence with a delicious menu influenced by French and Italian cooking, and sport due to its location at the foot of the Sugarbush ski and golf resort.

Above your bed is a blackboard covered in chalk-written algebraic formulae! Did Einstein once sleep here? In another suite, a chessboard painted on an old chest serving as a coffee table invites you to commence a strategic duel by the fireside. The Trout Room, eclectically decorated in a fishing theme, inspires all of its occupants to try their hand at fishing.

The Planters Inn is located in the very heart of Charleston's famed Historic District and was originally built in 1844.

Dating back three centuries, the City of Charleston is one of the best-preserved architectural treasures in the United States and is the birthplace of the Charleston dance – made famous by Josephine Baker. The meticulously restored colonial homes lining its charming streets are an eloquent reminder of its joyous and long history and the city still has all the charm that it owes to its multi-ethnic European origins. With their ornate landscaping and fountains, the courtyard and verandas of the Planters Inn create an urban oasis where guests can relax to a serenade of jazz, while sipping delicious cocktails and tasting the generous regional American cuisine of the nationally-acclaimed Peninsula Grill.

THE MAYFLOWER INN & SPA

118 Woodbury Road
Washington, Connecticut 06793
United States
Tel.:   + 1 860 868 9466
Fax: + 1 860 868 1497
E-mail: mayflower@relais.com
Website: www.relais.com/mayflower

THE PITCHER INN

275 Main Street, P.O. Box 347,
Warren, Vermont 05674
United States
Tel.:   + 1 802 496 6350
Fax: + 1 802 496 6354
E-mail: pitcher@relais.com
Website: www.relais.com/pitcher

PLANTERS INN

112 North Market Street
Charleston, South Carolina 29401
United States
Tel.:   + 1 843 722 2345
Fax: + 1 843 577 2125
E-mail: planters@relais.com
Website: www.relais.com/planters

THE POINT

THE RANCH AT ROCK CREEK

THE WAUWINET

The Point is a special place indeed set on the wooded shore of Upper Saranac Lake.

The Point, an Adirondack Great Camp, built for William A. Rockefeller, is a marvellous marriage of rustic simplicity and extraordinary luxury. Its eleven magnificent guest rooms are spread among four log buildings; here the silence and peace of the great North woods reign supreme. The Point is a study in delicious contrasts: the exceptional meals prepared by the kitchen, the blaze of the campfire on the edge of the dark lake, the fine art and antiques, most original to the camp, and the supply of snowshoes and skis for exploring the magical white forest. Enjoy gourmet picnic excursions, journeys through the rippling waters in gleaming mahogany boats, tasting menus of old cognacs, a staff that organizes each day according to the pleasure of the guests.

The Ranch at Rock Creek is a luxury guest ranch that brings together upscale amenities and wide open spaces like never before.

Set among 10 square miles of rugged Montana ranch land, guests experience limitless outdoor recreational opportunities, outstanding accommodations and cuisine, and a full-service spa. Families, couples and friends will discover that The Ranch at Rock Creek is a place that offers the feel of the 'true West' without sacrificing true comfort.

Built in 1860, The Wauwinet has the distinction of being one of the first hotels on the island of Nantucket.

With its tranquil harbors, endless stretches of beach, old manor houses, and beautiful gardens, the island of Nantucket is just 30 miles off the coast of Massachusetts. On the birthplace of Arthur Gordon Pym – hero of the novel of the same name by Edgar Allan Poe – stands The Wauwinet, a charming house covered in patinaed grey shingles. The freshly picked bunches of flowers in your room are characteristic of the attentiveness of the staff. Contemplate the splendid sunsets over Nantucket bay, relax or enjoy the water sports at the hotel's two private beaches, or indulge in massages inspired by local plants.

THE POINT

P.O. Box 1327
Saranac Lake, New York 12983
United States
Tel.:   + 1 518 891 5674
Fax: + 1 518 891 1152
E-mail: point@relais.com
Website: www.relais.com/point

THE RANCH AT ROCK CREEK

79 Carriage House Lane
Philipsburg, Montana 59858
United States
Tel.:   + 1 406 859 6027
Fax: + 1 406 859 6030
E-mail: rockcreek@relais.com
Website: www.relais.com/rockcreek

THE WAUWINET

120 Wauwinet Road, P.O. Box 2580
Nantucket, Massachusetts 02584
United States
Tel.:   + 1 800 426 8718
Fax: + 1 508 228 6712
E-mail: wauwinet@relais.com
Website: www.relais.com/wauwinet

WICKANINNISH INN

TRIPLE CREEK RANCH

TWIN FARMS

Blessed with a fabulous panoramic view, the Wickaninnish Inn is situated on a rocky outcropping in Tofino, on the West Coast of Vancouver Island.

Standing between the Pacific Ocean, Chesterman beach and a forest of giant evergreens, the design of the hotel's two buildings was entrusted to several artists, including the late celebrated wood carver Henry Nolla. The aim was to blend art, nature and culture. With big picture windows, the rooms offer grandiose views of the waves breaking on the shore and feature adzed cedar wood mantles and stone fireplaces. After a plant or marine-based treatment and an initiation to sea kayaking, you could even set off to see pods of whales just offshore.

The pleasures may change with the seasons but the program is always intense at Triple Creek Ranch.

In Summer, slip your boots into the stirrups, don your cowboy hat and set off to explore the rugged scenery of Montana with its white water torrents, conifers and prairies full of wild flowers. In Winter, put on your skis and glide down the slopes of the Rockies or enjoy a romantic couple's massage. The homemade cookies are a small clue to the hospitality of William and Leslie McConnell and the way they will look after you during your stay. An exceptional address that immerses you in the wild America of Westerns, and offers an intense moment of excitement for those who dare to go rafting down the Salmon River – the famous 'River of No Return'.

Twin Farms is an intimate, all-inclusive country hideaway set amidst 300 acres of meadows and woodlands in an unspoiled valley, 15 minutes north of Woodstock.

Hand-painted murals, rich maple and pine woodwork, American folk art and museum-quality contemporary oils adorn the rustically elegant accommodations and lounges. Public areas include the Dining Room, Barn Room, Pub, Cabana and Fitness Center. Twenty distinctive lodgings (including a self-contained four-suite 'Farmhouse at Copper Hill' overlooking a pond) feature king-size feather beds and sitting areas with wood-burning fireplaces that open onto screened porches. Whimsical cottages are tucked away in the property's secluded woodlands

The exceptional cuisine is backed by a 26,000-bottle wine cellar. On-site activities include hiking, biking, tennis, pond swimming, fly fishing and canoeing during the warmer months. Golf is available nearby. In winter, guests enjoy private downhill ski slopes, trails for cross-country skiing and snowshoeing as well as ice skating and sledding with all equipment provided. The property also offers a fitness center, Japanese-style soaking tub (Furo) and the Out of the Woods spa.

WICKANINNISH INN

Osprey Lane at Chesterman Beach, P.O. Box 250
Tofino, British Columbia V0R 2Z0
Canada
Tel.:   + 1 250 725 31 00
Fax: + 1 250 725 31 10
E-mail: wickaninnish@relais.com
Website: www.relais.com/wickaninnish

TRIPLE CREEK RANCH

5551 West Fork Road
Darby, Montana 59829
United States
Tel.:   + 1 406 821 4600
Fax: + 1 406 821 4666
E-mail: triplecreek@relais.com
Website: www.relais.com/triplecreek

TWIN FARMS

452 Royalton Turnpike
Barnard, Vermont 05031
United States
Tel.:   + 1 802 234 9999
Fax: + 1 802 234 9990
E-mail: twinfarms@relais.com
Website: www.relais.com/twinfarms

VILLA MARIA CRISTINA

WEDGEWOOD HOTEL & SPA

WESTGLOW RESORT AND SPA

An antique household turned into a luxury hotel the Villa Maria Cristina is a an oasis of peace and tranquility in the heart of Guanajuato.

The hallways simulate the alleys, as well as the patios and romantic corners found all over the city, lanterns and balconies, along with others decorative elements give an example of the 'Porfirian' era lived in the country over a century ago. Guests can relax surrounded by the sound of an Italian opera or soft classical music under an almost hand-painted blue sky, and the beautiful nights with amazing lighting, will give you a unique experience and grateful pleasure during your stay. Guests may also appreciate the amazing Bufa hill, well known throughout the whole 'Bajio' area, from the Jacuzzi located on the top terrace, while enjoying cocktails and delicious appetizers brought by our excellent chef.

This is a superb address set in the heart of the cosmopolitan city of Vancouver in fashionable Robson Square.

The lounges, resplendent with understated luxury, feature stylish furniture, rich fabrics and original fireplaces – all the personal vision of Eleni Skalbania who has decorated her property with timeless European elegance. The guest rooms reflect the perfect combination of ultimate modern comfort, antiques and original works of art, while the restaurant, dedicated to Bacchus, features inventive, highly epicurean cuisine. Today, every member of Eleni's staff, from the team at the splendid Spa to the chef in the restaurant, shares her quest for perfection and attention to detail.

Slip into luxury at one of the world's top all inclusive spa resorts in the beautiful Blue Ridge Mountains of North Carolina.

A boutique property in the heart of a fabulous, 42 acre estate, Westglow Resort and Spa, the former residence of the famous artist and author Elliott Daingerfield, is situated around an elegant mansion with panoramic views of the Blue Ridge Mountains in North Carolina. Exquisite accommodations include impeccably decorated guest rooms in the elegantly restored Greek Revival mansion. The award-winning spa provides an extensive array of indulgent treatments. The restaurant, Rowland's, offers sophisticated cuisine in an elegant setting. A unique atmosphere that combines nostalgia, sumptuousness and modernity will delight discerning travelers.

VILLA MARIA CRISTINA
Paseo de la Presa 76
Guanajuato 36000
Mexico
Tel.:   + 11 47 3731 2182
Fax: + 11 47 3731 2185
E-mail: cristina@relais.com
Website: www.relais.com/cristina

WEDGEWOOD HOTEL & SPA
845 Hornby Street
Vancouver, British Columbia V6Z 1V1
Canada
Tel.:   + 1 604 689 7777
Fax: + 1 604 608 5348
E-mail: wedgewood@relais.com
Website: www.relais.com/wedgewood

WESTGLOW RESORT AND SPA
224 Westglow Circle
Blowing Rock, North Carolina 28605
United States
Tel.:   + 1 843 295 4463
Fax: + 1 843 295 5115
E-mail: westglow@relais.com
Website: www.relais.com/westglow

THE WHITE BARN INN AND SPA

WINDHAM HILL INN

WINVIAN

Jonathan Cartwright is a respected and dedicated chef, who has turned the White Barn Inn into a truly great restaurant as well as a peaceful, elegant place to stay and a unique center of relaxation.

As a young boy he wanted to be a champion cyclist, but at the age of 15 he discovered cooking and his ambitions switched from wearing a yellow jersey to wearing a chef's whites. "Cooking requires the same determination as cycling, the same effort and the same team spirit," says this passionate perfectionist. Above all, Jonathan values the quality of his products and he can tell you the life story of the fresh Kennebunkport lobster, star of his menu, from its birth to the moment it arrives in his kitchen. To be savoured as it is, or in a bisque, or with a Cognac sauce, among the other creations inspired by local produce.

Welcome to Windham Hill, a romantic place where the summer nights offer up a magical spectacle and fall reveals all the glorious colors of nature.

At the end of a country road, in the heart of 160 hectares of unspoilt nature, this graceful inn offers you exceptional views of the Green Mountains. Stroll among the pine and maple trees, watch the fireflies when night falls in the rolling hills of Vermont, admire the star-filled skies in the moonlight. Windham Hill Inn offers a haven of peace with its elegant rooms and suites and a cuisine showcasing seasonal produce from the garden that is sure to delight the most discerning of gourmets.

Winvian is just two hours away from the buzz of New York and Boston. Within the green valleys and pristine lakes of the bucolic Litchfield Hills, Winvian is a unique hotel complex nestled in 45 hectares of lush grounds bordered by centuries-old maple trees.

A team of 15 architects was called upon to create the 19 original chalets, each with its own special design and atmosphere. Choose to stay in a 2 story treehouse perched 10 meters off the ground, in a lighthouse located in the midst of the forest, or perhaps a lodge built around a 100-year-old oak tree. On the agenda: relaxing in the romantic spa adjacent to the White Memorial nature preserve and Charles's pond, hot air ballooning, bike riding, croquet, bocce, horseback riding, fly fishing, race car driving among other unforgettable experiences.

THE WHITE BARN INN AND SPA

37 Beach Avenue
Kennebunk Beach, Maine 04043
United States
Tel.:   + 1 207 967 2321
Fax: + 1 207 967 1100
E-mail: whitebarn@relais.com
Website: www.relais.com/whitebarn

WINDHAM HILL INN

311 Lawrence Drive
West Townshend, Vermont 05359
United States
Tel.:   + 1 802 874 4080
Fax: + 1 802 874 4702
E-mail: windham@relais.com
Website: www.relais.com/windham

WINVIAN

155 Alain White Road
Morris, Connecticut 06763
United States
Tel.:   + 1 860 567 9600
Fax: + 1 860 567 9660
E-mail: winvian@relais.com
Website: www.relais.com/winvian

CONVERSIONS

Conversion Chart Weight (Solids)

¼ oz	7 g
½ oz	10 g
¾ oz	20 g
1 oz	25 g
1½ oz	40 g
2 oz	50 g
2½ oz	60 g
3 oz	75 g
3½ oz (1 cup)	100 g
4 oz (¼ lb)	110 g
4½ oz	125 g
5½ oz	150 g
6 oz	175 g
7 oz (2 cups)	200 g
8 oz (½ lb)	225 g
9 oz	250 g
10 oz	275 g
10½ oz (3 cups)	300 g
11 oz	310 g
11½ oz	325 g
12 oz (¾ lb)	350 g
13 oz	375 g
14 oz (4 cups)	400 g
15 oz	425 g
1 lb	450 g
18 oz	500 g (½ kg)
1¼ lb	600 g
1½ lb	700 g
1 lb 10 oz	750 g
2 lb	900 g
2¼ lb	1 kg
2½ lb	1.1 kg
2 lb 12 oz	1.2 kg
3 lb	1.3 kg
3 lb 5 oz	1.5 kg
3½ lb	1.6 kg
4 lb	1.8 kg
4 lb 8oz	2 kg
5 lb	2.25 kg
5 lb 8 oz	2.5 kg
6 lb 8 oz	3 kg

Volume (Liquids)

1 teaspoon (tsp)	5 ml
1 dessertspoon	10 ml
1 tablespoon (tbsp)	15 ml or ½ fl oz
1 fl oz	30 ml
1½ fl oz	40 ml
2 fl oz	50 ml
2½ fl oz	60 ml
3 fl oz	75 ml
3½ fl oz	100 ml
4 fl oz	125 ml
5 fl oz	150 ml or ¼ pint (pt)
5½ fl oz	160 ml
6 fl oz	175 ml
7 fl oz	200 ml
8 fl oz	225 ml
9 fl oz	250ml (¼ litre)
10 fl oz	300 ml or ½ pint
11 fl oz	325 ml
12 fl oz	350 ml
13 fl oz	370 ml
14 fl oz	400 ml
15 fl oz	425 ml or ¾ pint
16 fl oz	450 ml
18 fl oz	500 ml (½ litre)
19 fl oz	550 ml
20 fl oz	600 ml or 1 pint
1¼ pints	700 ml
1½ pints	850 ml
1¾ pints	1 litre
2 pints	1.2 litres
2½ pints	1.5 litres
3 pints	1.8 litres
3½ pints	2 litres
1 qt	950 ml
2 qt	1 litre
3 qt	2 litres
4 qt	3 litres
5 qt	4 litres

Oven Temperatures

Farenheit	Celsius *	Gas	Description
225°F	110°C	Gas Mark ¼	Cool
250°F	120°C	Gas Mark ½	Cool
275°F	130°C	Gas Mark 1	Very low
300°F	150°C	Gas Mark 2	Very low
325°F	160°C	Gas Mark 3	Low
350°F	180°C	Gas Mark 4	Moderate
375°F	190°C	Gas Mark 5	Moderate, Hot
400°F	200°C	Gas Mark 6	Hot
425°F	220°C	Gas Mark 7	Hot
450°F	230°C	Gas Mark 8	Very hot
475°F	240°C	Gas Mark 9	Very hot

Length

¼ inch (")	5 mm
½ inch	1 cm
¾ inch	2 cm
1 inch	2½ cm
1¼ inches	3 cm
1½ inches	4 cm
2 inches	5 cm
3 inches	7½ cm
4 inches	10 cm
6 inches	15 cm
7 inches	18 cm
8 inches	20 cm
10 inches	24 cm
11 inches	28 cm
12 inches	30 cm

* For fan assisted ovens, reduce temperatures by 10'C

Temperature conversion

C=5/9 (F-32)

F=9/5C+32

All preparation and cooking times are intended as a guide.

APPLE

Apple Cider Donuts 14

Apples with Crispy Maple Bread, Cranberry Sorbet, Green Tomato Confit, Yogurt Sauce, Cider Jelly & Cider Caramel 232

Golden Star Apple Beignet, Rose Hip Coulis, Fromage Blanc Glace 82

Hudson Valley Apple Pie 22

Vermont Apple Clafoutis with Wild Ginger & Vanilla Gelato Float 268

Warm Granny Smith Apple Tart with Cheddar Cheese Ice Cream 130

BANANA

Banana Cake 264

Banana Tart with Crème Chantilly 54

Flambéed Banana Panna Cotta & its Brunoise, New Brunswick Maple Sugar, Julienne Mint & Roasted Pecans 148

Maple Parfait, Blackberries & Banana Fritters 168

BISCUIT

Trio of Cookies 296

Vanilla Bean Biscuits with Mint & Basil Macerated Strawberries 220

BLACKBERRY

Maple Parfait, Blackberries & Banana Fritters 168

Warm Palisade Peach & Blackberry Cobbler 106

BLUEBERRY

Baked Lemon Pudding with Sour Cream Custard, Blueberry & Port Compote 276
Blueberry Cobbler 118

Maine Blueberry Crumble with Vanilla Cream 284

Olive Oil Cake with Blueberry Compote & Lemon Curd 248

BOURBON

Peach Cobbler with Bourbon Chantilly Cream 280

CAKE

Banana Cake 264

Black Plum Upside-down Cake 30

Chocolate Hazelnut Cake with Caramel Whipped Cream 212

Doberge Cake 126

Jean-George's Chocolate Cake 144

Olive Oil Cake with Blueberry Compote & Lemon Curd 248

Peninsula Grill Coconut Cake 208

Roasted Pineapple, Exotic Fruit, Almond Cake, Coconut Ice Cream 196

Tiramisu 38

Tres Leches Cake with Dulce de Leche, Kahlua & Oaxacan Mocha Chocolate 148

CARAMEL

Chocolate Hazelnut Cake with Caramel Whipped Cream 212

Mexican Rice Pudding with Caramel Sauce 74

Roast Caramel Pears with Gingerbread, Nutmeg Ice Cream Truffles 90

CHAMPAGNE

Little Red Berries with Champagne Sabayon 228

CHEESECAKE

Key Lime Cheesecake with Berry Compote 260

CHERRY

Port Cherries 184

CHESTNUTS

Spezzata di Castagne with Zested Mascarpone 62

CHOCOLATE

Canoe Bay's Baked Hot Chocolate with Mocha Foam 34

Chocolate Tart with Mandarin & Beets 288

Chocolate Pudding Pie 244

Jean-George's Chocolate Cake 144

Milk Chocolate Crémeux 152

Miniature Chocolate Baked Alaska 134

Mexican Hot Chocolate with Homemade Marshmallows 256

Warm Chocolate Tart with Maple & Hazelnut Ice Cream 18

CHURROS

Caribbean 'Chaudeau' & Churros 122

Mexican Churros 78

CIDER

Apple Cider Donuts 14

Apples with Crispy Maple Bread, Cranberry Sorbet, Green Tomato Confit, Yogurt Sauce, Cider Jelly & Cider Caramel 232

COBBLER

Blueberry Cobbler 118

Peach Cobbler with Bourbon Chantilly Cream 280

Warm Palisade Peach & Blackberry Cobbler 106

COCONUT

Fresh Coconut Flan 164

Peninsula Grill Coconut Cake 208

Roasted Pineapple, Exotic Fruit, Almond Cake, Coconut Ice Cream 196

COFFEE

Affogato 172

Canoe Bay's Baked Hot Chocolate with Mocha Foam 34

Tres Leches Cake with Dulce de Leche, Kahlua & Oaxacan Mocha Chocolate 148

CRANBERRY

Apples with Crispy Maple Bread, Cranberry Sorbet, Green Tomato Confit, Yogurt Sauce, Cider Jelly & Cider Caramel 232

Girly Cranberries 236

CREAM

Banana Tart with Crème Chantilly 54

Chocolate Hazelnut Cake with Caramel Whipped Cream 212